Instant Pot Cookbook

The Complete Instant Pot Cookbook - Delicious and Simple Recipes for your Instant Pot Pressure Cooker

Table of Contents

INTRODUCTION

If you're reading this book I'm guessing you've recently joined the Instant Pot club! The Instant Pot is the kind of appliance that people love, cherish, and rave about to their friends once they realize just how convenient and helpful it truly is.

In this book, you will find some brief tips and information on how to use your Instant Pot so you can get straight into experimenting with all kinds of dishes.

The recipe section is full of easy, healthy, and delicious recipes you can partially or entirely make in your Instant Pot. You will find recipes for: meat, poultry, seafood, vegan & vegetarian, breakfast, appetizers, and desserts.

There are no exotic or hard-to-find ingredients in these recipes, everything can be found from your local supermarket (or Asian food store in some cases). What's more, these recipes are very forgiving when it comes to substitutes, changes, and additions! In other words: use what you can, use what you have, use what you like!

Chapter 1: The Instant Pot

What is the Instant Pot?

The Instant Pot is an electric pressure cooker which can be used to cook many kinds of dishes at various temperatures, pressures, time frames, and cooking styles. The Instant Pot is not just a pressure cooker, it's also a rice cooker, slow cooker, and in some cases, a yoghurt maker!

The Instant Pot does not sit on the stove like a regular pot, it sits on the bench, out of the way. You can tuck your IP into the corner, next to a power outlet, ready to use whenever you need to create a quick (or slow-cooked!) meal.

You can't really make a mistake when using the Instant Pot, as the control pad has clearly-labelled buttons for each function, and a digital screen which tells you the temperature, time, and pressure selected. You can adjust the time, pressure, and temperature to suit your dish.

The functions you will find on most Instant Pot models are:

- Sauté
- Slow cooker
- Rice cooker
- Steam
- Poultry
- Soups
- Stews
- Beans/chili
- Multigrain
- Yogurt maker

Take a read through the manual you will have received with your Instant Pot, so you can become familiar with the buttons and functions your particular pot has to offer.

Benefits: why use it?

Cuts down kitchen time

It's all very well to prepare a roast dinner for your family in the middle of the week...but many people just don't have the time! That's where the Instant Pot is a true lifesaver. You can throw a whole chicken or leg of lamb into the pot and have dinner on the table (veggies and gravy included!) within the hour. And roasts are just one example. Soups, stews, chili, rice, oatmeal...all of these dishes and more can be prepared and cooked in a fraction of the time it would take with regular cooking methods.

Takes care of itself

Being able to walk away from the kitchen and leave your meal as it cooks is a total godsend. Once you have loaded the pot with ingredients, selected the function and time, you can pretty much abandon the pot while it does its thing. This is fabulous news for people who don't enjoy hanging out in the kitchen, or simply have too much else to do.

Doesn't clutter the stove

I love how you don't actually have to make a mess at all when you use the Instant Pot. You don't have to clutter and dirty the stove with pots and pans, and the bench can remain clear except for your classy and elegant Instant pot. All you need to do to clean up is rinse out the IP's inner pot, or throw it in the dishwasher! This will really appeal to neat-freaks and lazy cooks!

King of the one-pot meal

Ahh, the one-pot meal. Soups, stews, bakes, pot roasts, even pasta dishes! They can all be cooked in ONE pot. The versatility of one-pot meals makes it easy to increase your intake of veggies, fiber, and protein. Need more greens? Throw them into the pot for a one-pot pasta dish. Lacking in red meat and fiber? Pile some stewing meat and lentils into the pot for a hearty and wholesome one-pot stew. You get the idea! When time and creativity fail you: go for the one-pot Instant Pot meal.

Safe and sanitary food

Because the Instant Pot heats the food to such a high level of heat and pressure, no bugs (bacteria or viruses) can survive. Safe and hygienic food always gets two ticks and a big thumbs-up from me!

How to use it

Using the Instant Pot is extremely easy, but here are some quick guidelines to help you along the way. If you ever get stuck, simply refer to your manual or take a quick look at the Instant Pot website.

Load the pot

Place your ingredients into the pot, but remember not to overfill it! Only fill the pot 2 thirds full. You need to leave enough room for that great pressure, steam, and heat to cook your food evenly and thoroughly.

Use liquid

Because the IP uses steam to increase the pressure and heat, you must add liquid every time you use the pot. For dishes such as soup and stew, there's no need to worry, as you'll be adding plenty of liquid as part of the recipe. However, with roasts and dry meat dishes, remember to add at least a cup of water or stock to the pot.

Choose your function button

Decide what you are going to cook, and choose the function that bests suits your dish. For example: chicken drumsticks? Press the Poultry button. Pumpkin soup? Press the Soup button. Steamed veggies? Press the Steam button. You get it! If you're not quite sure which category your dish comes under, just choose the function which best fits the description, or simply use the Manual button to choose the temperature and time.

Adjust the time

Use the + and − buttons to adjust the cooking time. The function buttons each have a default time, and a lower and higher time to adjust to. You can also use the Manual button to choose very specific time frames.

Secure the lid onto the pot

Twist the lid onto the pot by using the arrows to guide you. You'll know you've done it right when the pot sings to you! Make sure you check the steam valve. If you are using the Slow Cook function, ensure that the steam valve is open ('venting'), otherwise, make sure it's closed 'sealing'.

Release the pressure: natural or quick

When the pot has finished cooking your meal (the time frame you chose has run out), you can either quick-release the pressure, or leave the pot to release the pressure naturally. When quick-releasing, cover your hand with a tea towel, and stand away from the jet of steam. All you need to do is switch the valve from 'sealing' to 'venting'. Don't worry, the Instant Pot will not allow you to take the lid off until all of the pressure has been released! No need to be scared of explosions and flying lids.

Don't overcook

Remember: The Instant Pot cooks most things at a far quicker rate than conventional cooking methods. Keep this in mind when choosing your cook-times, as you don't want to end up with overcooked food. Follow the time frames of these recipes and you'll be fine! Otherwise, a quick internet search of pressure cooker cook times comes in handy (what would we do without the internet, right?).

Chapter 2: Instant Pot Recipes

About these recipes

Salt and pepper: I haven't added salt and pepper in the list of ingredients for each recipe, as I think most people have salt and pepper ready to go in the kitchen. Also, salt and pepper are quite dependent on taste and preference, so I've left it up to you to add the amounts you like. When a recipe instruction states to "add salt and pepper", start with a small pinch, taste, then add more until your desired level of seasoning has been achieved.

Dried mixed herbs: lots of the savory recipes include dried mixed herbs in the ingredients list. I am referring to the generic "mixed herbs" packet you can find in all supermarkets, which most people have sitting in their cupboard. It doesn't matter which herbs your mixed herbs packet includes (they can slightly differ), so just use what you've got! Most mixed herbs include all or some of these herbs: oregano, thyme, basil, marjoram, and sage.

Sauté function: many of these recipes use the SAUTE function, it's just so extremely handy! The recipes tell you which temperature setting to use: low, normal, or high. The SAUTE function's default temperature is NORMAL. Remember: never put the lid on the pot when using the sauté function.

Approximate time: the time stated at the start of each recipe does NOT include the time the pot takes to come to pressure and heat. It refers only to the preparation and actual cooking time. You will get the hang of this once you start cooking with your Instant Pot! You'll get used to the pot heating up and coming to pressure and you can allow for the extra time.

Servings: the serving section at the start of each recipe is a rough idea of the amount of people the recipe will serve. This changes according to serving sizes of course!

Quick-releasing the pressure: most of these recipes state to quick-release the pressure and heat. Be careful when you do this! Carefully read your Instant Pot manual before you do your first "quick-release". Of course, if you're not there when the dish finishes cooking, just let the pot release naturally, it might just mean the dish inside continues to cook a little while longer.

Steaming baskets, trivets, and racks: many of these recipes call for the use of a steaming basket, a trivet, or a rack. Use the equipment you received with your Instant Pot, or if you've lost them (it happens!) use any other heat-proof equipment you have. When steaming, make sure the basket hangs above the water by placing the sides on the inner edges of the pot. The purpose of the trivet is to hold bowls and dishes above the bottom of the pot, and above the water, (like a little podium). The rack is used for things such as mini pies and cakes, as it allows the heat to circulate all around the dish without coming into contact with the bottom of a pot. Think of it like a mini oven rack.

Meat

These meat recipes are easy and very versatile. Some of them can be used for various different meals; the pork and fennel meatballs could be used on skewers, with noodles, or in a pita bread. The pulled pork with apple would make a great taco filling, or alone with a side of crispy potatoes. Get creative and use these recipes as inspiration for exciting and simple dinners!

Slow-Cooked Beef Stew for Rainy Nights

A rich beef stew with soft and starchy vegetables is the perfect way to comfort yourself after a long, cold, and wintry day. Place everything into the Instant Pot in the morning, so you can return home to a ready-to-go meal. This stew is very healthy, so even though it's comforting, it won't ruin any efforts to stick to a healthy diet.

Serves: 6
Time: approximately 8 hours

Ingredients:
- 2.5 lb stewing beef, diced and tossed in 2tbsp plain flour
- 2 onions, roughly chopped
- 6 garlic cloves, finely chopped
- 4 carrots, peeled and chopped into chunks
- 4 large potatoes, washed and chopped into chunks
- 2 parsnips, peeled and chopped into chunks
- 1 cup (8fl oz) red wine
- 4 cups (34fl oz) beef stock

Method:
1. Drizzle some olive oil into the Instant Pot and press the SAUTE button, keep the temperature at NORMAL.
2. Add the floured beef cubes and sauté for about 5 minutes or until browned.
3. Add the garlic and onions, sauté for about 3 minutes or until the onions are soft.
4. Add the carrots, potatoes, parsnips, wine, beef, salt, and pepper, stir to combine.
5. Secure the lid onto the Instant Pot and press the SLOW COOK button, adjust the time to 8 hours, and adjust the temperature to LOW, make sure the steam valve is open.
6. Once the pot beeps remove the lid and stir the stew.
7. Enjoy your hot, comforting stew!

Rosemary and Garlic Lamb Leg

A leg of lamb, cooked in the Instant Pot with garlic and fresh rosemary – absolutely delicious. Serve with any vegetables you like! A side of roasted potatoes never goes astray. Enjoy leftover cold meat the next day, in a sandwich or with a simple salad.

Serves: makes 1 leg of lamb, about 10 servings
Time: approximately 1 hour

Ingredients:
- 4.5 lb leg of lamb
- 2 onions, roughly chopped
- 8 garlic cloves, skin on, crushed with the back of a knife
- 2 large sprigs of fresh rosemary
- 2 cups (16fl oz) lamb or beef stock

Method:
1. Rub the leg of lamb with olive oil, salt and pepper.
2. Press the SAUTE button on your Instant Pot and keep the temperature at NORMAL.
3. Once the pot is hot, add the leg of lamb to the pot and sear on all sides to seal (about 4 minutes all together).
4. Remove the lamb from the pot and set aside.
5. Place the chopped onions, half of the garlic cloves, and one sprig of rosemary into the pot, pour the stock into the pot.
6. Lay the lamb leg onto the onion mixture and place the remaining onions, garlic, and rosemary on top of the lamb leg.
7. Secure the lid onto the pot and press the MEAT/STEW button, adjust the time to 45 minutes.
8. Once the pot beeps, quick-release the pressure, remove the lid, and place the lamb leg on a board to rest for 10 minutes.
9. You can squeeze the garlic cloves out of their skins and use them with the onions and rosemary to create lovely gravy!
10. Carve and serve the lamb once rested.

Honey Ginger Pork

Honey and ginger compliment chunks of pork deliciously. You could serve as a starter by offering a dish of tender pork chunks with toothpicks, or you could serve over a pile of fluffy rice.

Serves: 5-6
Time: approximately 30 minutes

Ingredients:
- 3 lb pork, cut into cubes
- 1 onion, finely chopped
- 3 garlic cloves, finely chopped
- 2 tbsp grated fresh ginger
- 3 tbsp honey
- 1 tbsp soy sauce
- 1 cup (8fl oz) apple juice

Method:
1. Drizzle some olive oil into the Instant Pot and press the SAUTE button, keep the temperature to NORMAL.
2. Add the onion and garlic to the pot, sauté for a few minutes until the onions are soft.
3. Add the pork to the pot and sauté for a few minutes to brown the meat.
4. Add the ginger, honey, soy sauce, and apple juice, stir to combine.
5. Secure the lid onto the pot and press the MEAT/STEW button, adjust the time to 20 minutes.
6. Once the pot beeps, quick-release the pressure and remove the lid.
7. Serve while hot!

Pulled Pork with Apple

Pulled pork inside a soft-shell taco, bao bun, or on its own with a tangy salad is a true winner. Many people find heavier cuts of pork to be a bit rich, and pulled pork is the answer! It's light, full of flavor, and very easy to make. This recipe uses whole apples to flavor the meat, and they can be used to create a sweet sauce to accompany the meat.

Serves: 4-6 (4 large servings, 6 small servings)
Time: approximately 1 hour 20 minutes

Ingredients:
- 4 lb pork shoulder, cut into 4 pieces
- 2 apples (I use Granny Smith), cut in half
- 1 onion, roughly chopped
- 2 tsp ground paprika
- 1 tsp ground coriander
- 1 tsp chili powder
- 1 cup apple juice
- 2 tbsp soy sauce
- 1 tbsp apple cider vinegar

Method:
1. Press the SAUTE button on your Instant Pot and adjust the temperature to HIGH.
2. Rub the pork shoulder pieces with olive oil and salt.
3. Once the pot is hot, sear the pork pieces on all sides to seal and brown, remove from the pot and set aside.
4. Add the onions and apples to the pot and lay the pork pieces onto them.
5. Sprinkle the paprika, coriander, and chili powder onto the meat.
6. Pour the soy sauce, apple juice, and apple cider vinegar into the pot (avoid pouring it on top of the meat otherwise it will wash way the seasonings).
7. Secure the lid onto the pot and press the MEAT/STEW button, manually adjust the time to 60 minutes.
8. Once the pot beeps, allow the pressure to release naturally before removing the lid and taking the meat out of the pot.
9. Pull the pork with two forks.
10. You can use the onions and apples left over in the pot to create a lovely apple sauce by blitzing with a hand-held blender!

Beef and Mushroom Pie Filling

You don't have to use this recipe as a pie filling, but I have called it that because I highly recommend that you do! You could use it to fill a simple pastry case, pile mashed potatoes on top, or serve it by itself with a side of steamed greens for a healthy dinner.

Serves: makes enough for 1 large pie
Time: approximately 40 minutes

Ingredients:
- 3 lb beef (chuck steak works well), cut into cubes and tossed in 2tbsp plain flour
- 1 onion, finely chopped
- 3 garlic cloves, finely chopped
- 5 large Portobello mushrooms, finely sliced
- 1 cup (8fl oz) red wine
- 1 cup (8fl oz) beef stock
- 2 tsp mixed dried herbs (rosemary, thyme, oregano, sage)

Method:
1. Press the SAUTE button on your Instant Pot and keep the temperature at NORMAL.
2. Drizzle some olive oil into the pot and add the onions, garlic, and mushrooms, sauté until the onions and mushrooms are soft.
3. Push the vegetables to one side of the pot and add the floured meat, sauté for a few minutes to brown the meat.
4. Add the red wine and stir, reduce for about 5 minutes to boil the alcohol off the wine.
5. Add the herbs, beef stock, salt, and pepper, stir to combine.
6. Secure the lid onto the pot and press the MEAT/STEW button, keep the time at the default 35 minutes.
7. Once the pot beeps, either quick-release or allow the pressure to release naturally, remove the lid and stir the mixture.
8. Use to fill a pie...or serve however you wish!

Mild Lamb Curry

A simple lamb curry is perfect as a mid-week dinner for the whole family, and this one is mild enough to suit children and spice-shy eaters. Serve with freshly-cooked rice and a side of greens (I always have a side of greens, so I can't help suggesting them!).

Serves: 6
Time: approximately 50 minutes

Ingredients:
- 3 lb lamb, cut into cubes
- 1 onion, finely chopped
- 4 garlic cloves, finely chopped
- 1 tin chopped tomatoes
- 1 can full-fat coconut milk
- 3 tbsp mild curry paste (use any, but I think red or yellow curry paste works best)
- 2 cups (16fl oz) lamb stock

Method:
1. Press the SAUTE button on your Instant Pot and keep the temperature at NORMAL.
2. Drizzle some olive oil into the pot and add the onions, garlic, and curry paste, sauté until fragrant.
3. Add the lamb to the pot and sauté for a few minutes.
4. Add the tomatoes, coconut milk, and stock, stir to combine.
5. Secure the lid onto the pot and press the MEAT/STEW button, adjust the time to 20 minutes.
6. Once the pot beeps, quick-release or allow the pressure to release naturally before removing the lid and stirring the curry.
7. Serve while hot, with some fluffy rice!

Tomato and Meat Sauce (for Bolognese or Lasagna)

A meat sauce is absolutely crucial for every home cook! You can throw this rich sauce into a lasagna, pour it on spaghetti, or layer it with eggplants and potatoes for an easy veggie bake.

Serves: approximately 6
Time: approximately 40 minutes

Ingredients:
- 2.5 lbs minced beef
- 2 onions, finely chopped
- 6 garlic cloves, finely chopped
- 2 large carrots, peeled and chopped into small pieces
- ¾ cup (7fl oz) red wine
- 4 cups (34fl oz) tomato passata or tomato puree
- 1 tsp mixed dried herbs

Method:
1. Press the SAUTE button on your Instant Pot and keep the temperature at NORMAL.
2. Drizzle some olive oil into the pot and add the onions, carrots, and garlic, sauté until the onions are soft.
3. Add the red wine and simmer for a few minutes to boil off the alcohol.
4. Add the minced beef and cook for a few minutes to brown.
5. Add the tomato passata, herbs, salt, and pepper, stir to combine.
6. Secure the lid onto the pot and press the BEAN/CHILI button and keep the time to the default 30 minutes.
7. Once the pot beeps, quick-release or allow the pressure to release naturally before removing the lid and stirring the sauce.
8. Serve however you like! I like to stir it into spaghetti, with a sprinkling of parmesan cheese on top.

Pork Chili

Minced pork and kidney beans are the key ingredients in this easy and yummy chili. For an exciting and easy dinner, pick up some tortilla chips, Greek yoghurt, guacamole, and spicy salsa...voila! Pork chili nachos. You could even fill some plastic containers with chili and keep them in the freezer to pull out whenever you're too tired to cook!

Serves: 6
Time: approximately 40 minutes

Ingredients:
- 3 lb minced pork
- 2 onions, finely chopped
- 4 garlic cloves, finely chopped
- 2 tins kidney beans, drained
- 2 tins chopped tomatoes
- 1 tsp brown sugar
- 1 tsp ground paprika
- 1 tsp ground cumin
- 1 tsp ground coriander
- 1 tsp chili powder

Method:
1. Press the SAUTE button on your Instant Pot and keep the temperature at NORMAL.
2. Drizzle some olive oil into the pot and add the onions and garlic, sauté until the onions are soft.
3. Add the minced pork to the pot and sauté for a few minutes to brown the meat.
4. Add the beans, tomatoes, sugar, paprika, cumin, coriander, chilli, salt, and pepper to the pot, stir to combine.
9. Secure the lid onto the pot and press the BEAN/CHILI button and keep the time to the default 30 minutes.
10. Once the pot beeps, quick-release or allow the pressure to release naturally before removing the lid and stirring the hot chili.
5. Serve with any sides and toppings you fancy!

Lamb and Parsnip Casserole

Lamb and parsnips cook under pressure, becoming soft and rich. If you like, you can swap the parsnips for carrots or potatoes depending on what's in season and which veggie you like best! If you want to, you can also slow cook this recipe on low for 8 hours.

Serves: 6
Time: approximately 45 minutes

Ingredients:
- 3 lb lamb (a cheap stewing cut works fine), cut into cubes and tossed in 2tbsp plain flour
- 2 onions, roughly chopped
- 6 garlic cloves, finely chopped
- 1 tbsp tomato paste
- 4 parsnips, peeled and chopped into chunks
- 1 tsp ground paprika
- 4 cups (38fl oz) lamb stock

Method:
1. Press the SAUTE button on your Instant Pot and keep the temperature at NORMAL.
2. Drizzle some olive oil into the pot and add the onions and garlic, sauté until the onions are soft.
3. Add the lamb cubes and sauté for a few minutes to brown the meat.
4. Add the tomato paste, parsnips, paprika, stock, salt, and pepper, stir to combine.
5. Secure the lid onto the pot and press the MEAT/STEW button and keep the time to the default 35 minutes.
6. Once the pot beeps, quick-release or allow the pressure to release naturally before removing the lid and stirring the casserole.
7. Serve hot!

Lamb Chops with Fresh Herbs

To me, lamb chops are the best way to indulge in a comforting yet healthy meal. The fat content of lamb chops, and the meat close to the bone are so incredibly tasty and satisfying. This recipe uses fresh herbs to gently flavor the meat. Serve with any veggies you like.

Serves: makes 8 lamb chops
Time: approximately 20 minutes

Ingredients:
- 8 lamb chops
- 4 garlic cloves, crushed
- 1 sprig of fresh rosemary
- Small bunch of fresh mint
- Few sprigs of fresh thyme
- 1 cup (8fl oz) lamb stock

Method:
1. Press the SAUTE button on your Instant Pot and keep the temperature at NORMAL.
2. Drizzle some olive oil into the pot.
3. Once the oil is hot, sear the lamb chops on both sides for a minute or two, until browned.
4. Press the MEAT/STEW button and adjust the time to 10 minutes.
5. Rub the browned lamb chops with crushed garlic, salt, and pepper.
6. Pour the stock into the bottom of the pot and place a trivet into the pot.
7. Place the lamb chops onto the trivet, with the fresh herbs on top of the chops.
8. Secure the lid onto the pot and leave to cook.
9. Once the pot beeps, quick-release the pressure and remove the lid.
10. Serve the lamb chops with a drizzle of any leftover liquid from the pot!

Chili Beef Strips with Rice Noodles

This recipe is so easy to whip up, but it makes the most amazing dish. Cold rice noodles, rare beef strips, fresh chilli, and a hit of salty soy sauce. You can make this as a salad to bring to barbeques, or as a yummy Summertime dinner.

Serves: 6
Time: approximately 15 minutes

Ingredients:
- 2 large steaks, sirloin works well for this dish
- 2 lb rice noodles, I like to use the flat ones usually used for Pad Thai
- 1 garlic clove, crushed
- 1 fresh red chili, finely chopped
- 1 lime
- 2 tbsp soy sauce
- 1 tsp sesame oil

Method:
1. Cook the rice noodles according to the packet instructions, (some noodles only require boiling water to be poured over and left for a few minutes), run them under some cold water, then leave aside.
2. Press the SAUTE button on your Instant Pot and adjust the temperature to HIGH.
3. Rub the steaks with olive oil and pepper.
4. Place the steaks into the pot and cook on both sides for about 2 minutes each, (or cook to your desired doneness).
5. Once cooked, place the steaks on a board and leave to rest for about 10 minutes.
6. Before slicing the steaks, sprinkle them with salt (I don't put salt on the steaks before cooking as it can draw moisture out), slice into thin strips.
7. Assemble the salad by placing the noodles, crushed garlic, chopped chili, juice of the lime, soy sauce, and sesame oil into a large bowl, mix to combine.
8. Place the steak strips on top of the salad before serving, some fresh green herbs would look and taste lovely too!

Cheat's Lasagna with Lamb or Beef

I call this "cheat's" because it's very easy, and doesn't require any white sauce or boiling lasagna sheets. Of course, you can add white sauce if you like! But I find that a layer of ricotta cheese is lighter and healthier than buttery, floury (albeit delicious) white sauce. You can use lamb or beef!

Serves: 6 small servings
Time: approximately 55 minutes

Ingredients:
- 2 lb minced lamb or beef
- 1 onion, finely chopped
- 3 garlic cloves, finely chopped
- 2 carrots, peeled and chopped into small pieces
- 1 cup (8fl oz) red wine
- 2 cups (16fl oz) tomato passata or tomato puree
- 1 tsp mixed dried herbs
- 4 large sheets of pre-cooked lasagna sheets
- 14 oz ricotta cheese
- 10 oz grated mozzarella cheese

Method:
1. Press the SAUTE button on your Instant pot and keep the temperature at NORMAL.
2. Drizzle some olive oil into the pot and add the onions, garlic, and carrot, sauté until soft.
3. Add the minced meat to the pot and sauté for a few minutes until the meat has browned.
4. Add the red wine and simmer for a few minutes until the alcohol has been boiled off.
5. Add the tomato passata, dried herbs, salt and pepper, leave to simmer for about 20 minutes or until thick and reduced.
6. Preheat the oven to 374 degrees Fahrenheit and get a rectangular dish ready.
7. Spread some of the meat sauce onto the bottom of the dish, then layer with mozzarella sheets, ricotta, and meat sauce until all ingredients have been used up.
8. Complete the layering with a layer of ricotta cheese and the grated mozzarella on top.
9. Place into the oven and bake for about 35 minutes or until bubbling and the lasagna sheets are soft and cooked through.

Lamb and Mint Pies

Meat pies are an absolute classic in British, New Zealand, and Australian food traditions. If you're not used to eating meat pies...try this recipe! Hot lamb, fresh mint, and flaky pastry, with a dollop of ketchup on the top: YUM! You will need some individual pie tins for this recipe. Or, you could make them in muffin tins if you can't get pie tins.

Serves: makes 6 pies
Time: approximately 50 minutes

Ingredients:
- 2 lb minced lamb
- 1 onion, finely chopped
- 6 garlic cloves, finely chopped
- Small handful of fresh mint, finely chopped
- 1 lamb stock cube
- Store-bought puff pastry, enough for 6 pies
- 1 egg, lightly beaten

Method:
1. Preheat your oven to 374 degrees Fahrenheit.
2. Press the SAUTE button on your Instant Pot and keep the temperature at NORMAL.
3. Drizzle some olive oil into the pot and add the onion and garlic, sauté until soft.
4. Add the minced lamb to the pot and sauté for a few minutes until the meat has browned.
5. Add the mint, stock cube and 2 cups of hot water, stir to combine, allow the mixture to simmer for about 20 minutes until reduced and thick.
6. Prepare the pie tins by greasing them with butter and sprinkling with flour.
7. Lay the pastry over the pie tins and press into the edges so that the bottom of each tin is lined with pastry.
8. Fill each pastry case with the hot minced meat mixture.
9. Cut out rounds of pastry to place on top of each pie, and use a fork to seal the pastry, prick the top of each pie to allow steam to escape when cooking.
10. Brush the top of each pie with the beaten egg.
11. Place the pies into the oven and cook for about 20 minutes or until golden brown!

Soy and Sesame Beef Ribs

These beef ribs are salty, nutty, sticky, and addictive. Cook up a batch next time you have guests around, or are heading out to a pot luck party.

Serves: 6
Time: approximately 1 hour

Ingredients:
- 4 lb beef ribs
- 3 tbsp soy sauce
- 1 tbsp sesame oil
- 1 tbsp sesame seeds
- 1 tbsp honey
- 1 cup (8fl oz) beef stock

Method:
1. In a large bowl, place the ribs, soy sauce, sesame oil, sesame seeds, honey, and beef stock, stir to combine and coat the ribs in sauce.
2. Pour the contents of the bowl into the Instant Pot, including all of the liquid.
3. Secure the lid onto the pot and press the MEAT/STEW button, adjust the time to 45 minutes.
4. Once the pot beeps, quick-release the pressure, remove the lid, and place the ribs onto a dish with a generous drizzle of leftover liquid.

Pork and Fennel Seed Meatballs

Fennel seeds are available from all supermarkets, and they have a gorgeous aniseed-like flavor. These pork meat balls are great when served with tooth picks as a starter, in a pita bread, or with spaghetti!

Serves: makes about 30 meatballs
Time: approximately 30 minutes

Ingredients:
- 4 lb minced pork
- 6 garlic cloves, crushed
- 2 eggs, lightly beaten
- 2 tbsp almond meal
- 2 tsp fennel seeds

Method:
1. In a large bowl, add the minced pork, garlic, eggs, almond meal, fennel seeds, salt, and pepper, mix with your hands until fully combined.
2. Roll the mixture into 30 balls.
3. Press the SAUTE button on your Instant Pot and adjust the temperature to HIGH.
4. Drizzle some olive oil into the pot.
5. Once the oil is hot, add the meat balls to the pot in batches and fry for about 5 minutes, turning to ensure all sides are brown and golden.
6. Serve however you wish!

Poultry

The trusty chicken - a dinnertime favorite on tables all around the world. Whole chicken, thighs, breasts, wings, and drumsticks feature in this section, with many different flavors and cooking methods to explore. Try to buy free range chicken if you can!

Lemon and Rosemary Chicken Thighs

Chicken thighs carry much more flavor and juiciness than chicken breasts, so they make a lovely dinner when dressed in yummy flavors like lemon and rosemary. A simple salad and some roasted potatoes are all you need to put together an easy, healthy dinner.

Serves: 4
Time: approximately 15 minutes

Ingredients:
- 8 boneless chicken thighs
- 4 garlic cloves, finely chopped
- 2 lemons, cut in half
- 1 large sprig of fresh rosemary, or 1tsp dried rosemary
- 1 cup (8fl oz) chicken stock

Method:
1. Drizzle some olive oil into the Instant Pot and press the SAUTE button, keep the temperature at NORMAL.
2. Once the oil is hot, sauté the chicken thighs for about 1 minute on each side, until browned.
3. Add the garlic, rosemary, salt, pepper, stock, and juice of both lemons to the pot, add the lemon halves to the pot after you've squeezed them, stir to combine.
4. Secure the lid onto the pot and press the POULTRY button, adjust the time to 10 minutes.
5. Once the pot beeps, quick-release the pressure and remove the lid.
6. Serve the chicken thighs with a good spoonful of leftover lemony liquid from the pot.

Chicken Casserole with Root Vegetables and Sausage

With this recipe, you can use any combination of root vegetables you like, and any kind of sausage. I like to use carrots and sweet potatoes, and a delicious beef sausage from the butcher.

Serves: 6
Time: approximately 1 hour

Ingredients:
- 1 knob of butter
- 8 boneless chicken thighs
- 1 onion, finely chopped
- 5 garlic cloves, finely chopped
- 5 sausages, cut into chunks
- 3 carrots, cut into chunks
- 3 large sweet potatoes, cut into chunks
- 2 tbsp plain flour
- 1 tsp dried mixed herbs
- 4 cups (38lf oz) chicken stock

Method:
1. Press the SAUTE button on your Instant Pot and keep the temperature at NORMAL.
2. Add the butter and a drizzle of olive oil to the pot.
3. Once the pot is hot, add the chicken thighs to the pot and sauté on each side for about 1 minute each, to seal and brown the meat.
4. Add the garlic, onion, flour, herbs, salt, and pepper to the pot, stir to combine and coat the chicken.
5. Add the root veggies to the pot along with the chicken stock, stir to combine.
6. Secure the lid onto the pot and press the POULTRY button, adjust the time to 30 minutes.
7. Once the pot beeps, allow the pot to naturally release the pressure before removing the lid and stirring your lovely hot casserole!

Lime and Coconut Chicken

Tropical flavors of coconut and lime really give chicken a total makeover! I serve this dish with brown rice and steamed asparagus.

Serves: 4
Time: approximately 25 minutes

Ingredients:

- 8 boneless chicken thighs
- 1 onion, finely chopped
- 4 garlic cloves, finely chopped
- 2 limes
- 1 can full-fat coconut cream
- 1 cup (8fl oz) chicken stock
- 1 tsp chili flakes

Method:

1. Press the SAUTE button on your Instant pot, keep the temperature at NORMAL.
2. Drizzle some olive oil into the pot and add the onion and garlic, sauté until soft.
3. Add the chicken thighs to the pot and sauté on both sides until browned and sealed.
4. Add the coconut cream, stock, chili flakes, salt, pepper, and juice of both of the limes, stir to combine.
5. Secure the lid onto the pot and press the POULTRY button, keep the time at the default 15 minutes.
6. Once the pot beeps, allow the pressure to naturally release, remove the lid, and serve the chicken with a generous spoonful of coconut sauce!

Instant Pot Whole Chicken

A whole cooked chicken goes a very long way, either as a roast dinner, or to fill rolls and sandwiches for lunch. This recipe is extremely simple, but you can add your own flair by adding a rub or topping.

Serves: makes 1 whole chicken
Time: approximately 35 minutes

Ingredients:
- 1 whole chicken
- 1 lemon
- 1 cup (8fl oz) chicken stock

Method:
1. Press the SAUTE button on your Instant Pot and adjust the temperature to HIGH.
2. Drizzle some olive oil into the pot and sauté the chicken (topside down) for a few minutes to seal and brown the skin.
3. Remove the chicken from the pot and pour the stock into the pot.
4. Stuff the chicken's cavity with the lemon, and rub the top of the chicken with salt and pepper.
5. Place a trivet into the pot and place the chicken on top of it.
6. Secure the lid onto the pot and press the POULTRY button, adjust the time to 25 minutes.
7. Once the pot beeps, quick-release the pressure and place the chicken on a board to rest for about 10 minutes.

Duck Breast with Red Wine Sauce

Here's a fancier recipe for impressing dates or special guests. Duck breast is a delicious meat, and the red wine sauce makes it even more luxurious. Of course, you can use chicken breast instead.

Serves: 4
Time: approximately 40 minutes

Ingredients:
- Large knob of butter
- 4 duck breasts, skin on
- 4 garlic cloves, finely chopped
- 2 cups (18fl oz) red wine
- 1 tsp dried mixed herbs

Method:
1. Press the SAUTE button on your Instant Pot and keep the temperature at NORMAL.
2. Add the butter to the pot with a drizzle of olive oil.
3. Once the pot is hot, add the duck breasts, skin-side down, and sauté for about 3 minutes until the skin is golden and crispy.
4. Turn the breasts over and cook on the other side for about 12 minutes or until cooked all the way through.
5. Remove the breasts from the pot and leave to rest on a board, sprinkle with salt and pepper.
6. Make the sauce by adding the onion, garlic, and herbs to the pot, sauté until soft.
7. Add the red wine to the pot and simmer for about 8 minutes or until reduced and thick.
8. Serve the duck breasts with a generous serving of red wine sauce over top!

Butter Chicken Drumsticks

Creamy butter chicken is a Westernized Indian dish made from butter, cream tomatoes, and spices. This recipe uses drumsticks and a mild sauce. Serve with a fresh salad and some fluffy naan breads!

Serves: 4
Time: approximately 40 minutes

Ingredients:
- 8 chicken drumsticks
- 4 garlic cloves, crushed
- 1 tbsp grated fresh ginger
- 1 tsp ground cumin
- 1 tsp ground coriander
- 1 tsp chili powder
- 1 tsp ground paprika
- Small knob of butter
- 1 cup (8fl oz) tomato passata or puree
- 1 cup (8fl oz) heavy cream

Method:
1. Press the SAUTE button on your Instant Pot and keep the temperature at NORMAL.
2. Drizzle some olive oil into the pot.
3. Once the pot is hot, add the drumsticks to the pot and sauté on both sides for a few minutes, until golden and sealed.
4. Add the garlic, ginger, cumin, coriander, chili, paprika, butter, tomato passata, cream, salt, and pepper, stir to combine.
5. Secure the lid onto the pot and press the POULTRY button, keep the time at the default 15 minutes.
6. Once the pop beeps, quick-release the pressure, remove the lid, and serve your chicken drumsticks with plenty of butter chicken sauce!

Spicy Wings with Sour Cream Dipping Sauce

A big pile of spicy wings with sour cream dipping sauce is perfect for a party or games night! You can use drumsticks instead, for a more robust meal.

Serves: about 8 people as a starter or snack
Time: approximately 30 minutes

Ingredients:
- 3 lb chicken wings
- ½ cup (5floz) tomato puree
- 1 tbsp tabasco
- 2 tsp brown sugar
- ½ cup (5fl oz) chicken stock
- 1 cup sour cream
- ½ cup Greek yogurt
- 1 lime

Method:
1. In a large bowl, place the chicken wings, tomato puree, tabasco, brown sugar, chicken stock, salt, and pepper, stir to combine and coat the wings.
2. Press the POULTRY button on your Instant Pot and keep the time to the default 15 minutes.
3. Pour the contents of the bowl into the pot (including all of the sauce!).
4. Secure the lid onto the pot leave to cook.
5. Meanwhile, make the dipping sauce by combining the sour cream, yoghurt, and juice of the lime, add some salt and pepper to taste according to your preference.
6. Once the pot beeps, quick-release the pressure, remove the lid, and place your hot saucy wings onto a serving platter with the sour cream sauce on the side!

Italian-Style Chicken with Tomato and Olives

This recipe is inspired by a classic Italian dish Chicken Cacciatore. If you want to make it a bit more indulgent, you can add a layer of grated mozzarella cheese on top! Crusty bread and a fresh salad are great accompaniments to this dish.

Serves: 6
Time: approximately 40 minutes

Ingredients:
- 8 chicken boneless chicken thighs
- 2 tins chopped tomatoes
- 6 garlic cloves, finely chopped
- 1 onion, finely chopped
- 20 black olives, stones removed, chopped into quarters
- 2 tbsp capers (optional)
- 1 tsp dried oregano

Method:
1. Drizzle some olive oil into your Instant Pot and press the SAUTE button, keep the temperature at NORMAL.
2. Add the onions, garlic, and oregano to the pot, sauté for a few minutes until soft.
3. Add the chicken thighs to the pot and sauté on both sides for a minute or two until golden.
4. Add the tinned tomatoes, olives, capers, salt, and pepper to the pot, stir to combine.
5. Secure the lid onto the pot and press the POULTRY button, adjust the time to 30 minutes.
6. Once the pot beeps, quick-release the pressure, remove the lid, and serve hot!

Chicken and Veggie Sushi

Don't be intimidated by making sushi! You can buy nori (seaweed) in most supermarkets, and the rolling is actually really easy. These sushi rolls feature chicken, avocado, and carrot, but you can use any other veggies you like.

Serves: makes 5 sushi rolls (each roll can be cut into 6 pieces)
Time: approximately 45 minutes

Ingredients:
- 2 large chicken breasts, skin removed
- 2 tbsp soy sauce
- ½ cup (5fl oz) chicken stock
- 1 cup sushi rice
- 5 nori sheets
- 1 large avocado, stone removed, cut into 10 slices
- 1 large carrot, peeled and cut into long thin strips

Method:
1. Cook the sushi rice according to the packet instructions, (you can use the Instant Pot, but you'll just have to rinse it out afterwards so you can cook the chicken).
2. Place the chicken, soy sauce, and chicken stock into the Instant Pot and press the POULTRY button, keep the time to the default 15 minutes.
3. Secure the lid onto the pot and leave to cook.
4. Once the pot beeps, quick-release the pressure, remove the lid, and take the chicken out of the pot.
5. Slice the chicken into strips.
6. Lay a nori sheet onto a board or sushi mat.
7. Spread a layer of cooked sushi rice over the sheet, leaving a 1 inch gap at the top of the sheet.
8. Place some chicken, avocado and carrot along the width of the rice.
9. Roll the sushi tightly, and seal the end by rubbing some warm water along the loose edge.
10. Slice and serve with soy sauce!

Creamy Chicken Soup with Corn and Parsley

Creamy chicken soup with corn and fresh parsley, a yummy Winter dinner to greet you after work! You can pressure cook this soup on high for 25 minutes if you prefer, but this recipe uses the slow cook function.

Serves: 6-8
Time: approximately 8 hours

Ingredients:
- 2 chicken breasts, cut into small chunks
- 1 onion, finely chopped
- 5 garlic cloves, finely chopped
- 1 large potato, peeled and chopped into chunks
- 1 cup (8fl oz) heavy cream
- 4 cups (38fl oz) chicken stock
- 2 cups frozen or tinned corn kernels
- Handful of fresh parsley, finely chopped

Method:
1. Drizzle some olive oil into the Instant Pot and press the SAUTE button, keep the temperature at NORMAL.
2. Add the onion, garlic, chicken, salt, and pepper to the pot, sauté until the onions are soft and the chicken is beginning to turn golden.
3. Add the potato, cream, stock, and corn kernels to the pot.
4. Secure the lid onto the pot and press the SLOW COOK button, adjust the time to 8 hours.
5. Make sure the steam vent is closed.
6. Once the pot beeps, remove the lid and serve yourself a big bowl of hot, creamy soup with fresh parsley on top!

Chicken and Leek Bake

Leeks are such a delicious vegetable; they become soft and silky when cooked, and have a beautiful oniony flavor. This one-dish bake can be modified and changed to suit your tastes, and what's in season.

Serves: 6-8
Time: approximately 1 hour

Ingredients:
- 8 boneless chicken thighs
- 2 leeks, (green part removed) finely sliced
- 4 garlic cloves, finely chopped
- 1 large potato, peeled and thinly sliced
- 1 cup (8fl oz) chicken stock
- ½ cup (5fl oz) heavy cream
- 1 cup grated cheese (any cheese you like)

Method:
1. Drizzle some olive oil into your Instant Pot and press the SAUTE button, keep the temperature at NORMAL.
2. Once the pot is hot, brown the chicken thighs on both sides for a couple of minutes until golden.
3. Remove the chicken from the pot and add the garlic and leeks to the pot, sauté until soft.
4. In a pressure cooker-safe dish (make sure it fits into your Instant Pot) layer the chicken thighs, leek and garlic mixture, and potato slices.
5. Stir together the cream, stock, cheese, salt, and pepper, pour over the top of the dish and allow it to seep into the other ingredients for a couple of minutes.
6. Pour 1 cup of water into the Instant Pot and place the trivet into the pot.
7. Place the chicken and leek dish onto the trivet and secure the lid onto the Instant Pot.
8. Press the POULTRY button and adjust the time to 30 minutes.
9. Once the pot beeps, quick-release the pressure and remove the lid.
10. Carefully take the dish out and serve your yummy bake while hot!

Stuffed Chicken Breast

Chicken breast on its own can be a bit dry and boring, but not if you stuff it with delicious fillings! This recipe uses cream cheese, sundried tomatoes (a bit retro), and fresh basil. You can improvise with your fillings if you wish!

Serves: 6 (I find that 4 chicken breasts serve 6 people when sliced)
Time: approximately 35 minutes

Ingredients:
- 4 large skinless chicken breasts
- 2 garlic cloves, crushed
- 4 tbsp full-fat cream cheese
- ¼ cup sundried tomatoes, finely chopped
- About 8 fresh basil leaves

Method:
1. In a small bowl, combine the crushed garlic, cream cheese, sundried tomatoes, pepper, and a small drizzle of olive oil until smooth.
2. Cut a cavity into each chicken breast by slicing down the middle of the breast lengthways, but don't cut in half.
3. Stuff each breast's cavity with a heaped tablespoonful of the cream cheese mixture and 2 basil leaves.
4. To keep the breasts closed you can poke a toothpick through the center if you like.
5. Drizzle some olive oil into your Instant Pot and press the SAUTE button, keep the temperature at NORMAL.
6. Once the oil is hot, sear each breast on each side for a couple of minutes until golden.
7. Pour 1 cup of water into the Instant Pot and place a trivet into the pot, place the chicken breasts onto the trivet.
8. Secure the lid onto the pot and press the POULTRY button, adjust the time to 5 minutes.
9. Once the pot beeps, allow the pressure to release naturally before removing the lid and placing the stuffed breasts on a board to slice and serve!

Simple Shredded Chicken Breast for Chicken Salads and Sandwiches

Chicken salads and sandwiches need fresh, well-cooked chicken. Your Instant Pot allows you to prepare chicken quickly and safely, so you can whip up a salad or batch of sandwiches even if you're running completely behind schedule! There are no fancy additions or toppings with this recipe (except a humble lemon), but you can add rubs and marinades if you wish.

Serves: makes 3 chicken breasts, enough for a large salad or sandwiches for 6-8 people
Time: approximately 10 minutes

Ingredients:
- 3 skinless chicken breasts
- 1 lemon

Method:
1. Rub the chicken breasts with olive oil, salt, and pepper.
2. Pour 1 cup of water (or chicken stock if you have some on hand) into the Instant Pot.
3. Place a trivet into the pot and lay the chicken breasts on top of the trivet.
4. Slice the lemon into 9 thin slices and lay them on top of the chicken breasts.
5. Secure the lid onto the pot and press the POULTRY button, adjust the time to 10 minutes.
6. Once the pot beeps, quick-release the pressure and remove the lid.
7. Take the chicken breasts out of the pot and either slice them with a sharp knife, or shred with 2 forks.

Easy One-Pot Chicken Pasta

Anything which can be described as "one-pot" gets a huge tick from me, especially when pasta is involved. Chicken, cream, bacon, lemon, pasta, and parmesan cheese...yes, I know, it's not the healthiest meal on earth! But hey, we all deserve a decadent dinner sometimes.

Serves: 6
Time: approximately 15 minutes

Ingredients:
- 3 boneless chicken thighs, cut into small pieces
- 4 garlic cloves, crushed
- 4 cups dried pasta (any type of short pasta: penne, bowties, spirals, shells)
- 1 cup (8fl oz) heavy cream
- 2 cups (8fl oz) chicken stock
- 3 rashers streaky bacon, cut into small pieces
- 1 lemon, cut into quarters
- ½ cup grated parmesan cheese
- Fresh parsley to serve

Method:
1. Add the chicken, garlic, pasta, cream, stock, bacon, lemon quarters, salt, and pepper to the Instant Pot.
2. Stir to combine and make sure all of the pasta pieces are covered in liquid.
3. Secure the lid to the pot and press the MANUAL button, adjust the temperature to HIGH, and adjust the time for 7 minutes.
4. Once the pot beeps, allow the pressure to release naturally before removing the lid.
5. Stir the parmesan into the hot pasta dish and serve with a sprinkling of fresh parsley!

Chicken with Mango (Ideal for Tacos)

I can be a bit fussy when it comes to mixing fruit and meat (except lemon!), but one combination I can't get enough of is mango and chicken. This is an absolutely incredible taco filling, and it's also amazing served on top of coconut rice.

Serves: 6
Time: approximately 15 minutes

Ingredients:

- 6 boneless chicken thighs
- 1 large mango, peeled, flesh removed and cut into small pieces
- 4 garlic cloves, crushed
- 1 tsp chili flakes (or 1 fresh red chili, finely chopped)
- 1 lime
- 1 cup (8fl oz) chicken stock

Method:

1. Place the chicken, mango, garlic, chili, lime, stock, salt, and pepper to the Instant Pot, stir to combine.
2. Secure the lid onto the pot and press the POULTRY button, adjust the time to 30 minutes.
3. Once the pot beeps, quick-release the pressure and remove the lid.
4. Spoon the mango chicken onto a dish and pull the chicken with 2 forks.
5. Serve however you like!

Seafood

Seafood is quick to cook and full of nutritious properties. White fish, salmon, prawns, calamari, and crabmeat star in this section. Family favorites such as burgers and macaroni are given a fishy twist you will love! Buy fresh fish fillets from your local fish monger, or use high-quality frozen seafood.

Seared Salmon

Salmon is such a rich and delicious fish, full of oils to make your skin and hair glow. I think one of the best ways to serve salmon is to sear it on a hot surface with a sprinkle of salt and pepper, and serve with a side of in-season veggies.

Serves: 4

Time: approximately 10 minutes

Ingredients:
- 4 salmon fillets, skin on, bones removed
- 1 lemon
- Knob of butter

Method:
1. Drizzle some olive oil into the Instant Pot and press the SAUTE button, keep the temperature at NORMAL.
2. Rub the salmon with olive oil and sprinkle with salt and pepper.
3. Slice the lemon into 8 slices.
4. Place the salmon skin-side down into the hot pot and lay the lemon slices on top of the fillets.
5. Cook the salmon for about 5 minutes, or until you see that the salmon has cooked almost all the way through.
6. Remove the lemon slices and place a small knob of butter on top of each fillet before serving, it will melt onto the salmon and create a light, buttery, and lemony sauce!

One-Pot Prawn Pasta

Just like the one-pot chicken pasta, this prawn version is just as quick and easy! Frozen prawns are perfectly fine to use.

Serves: 6
Time: approximately 20 minutes

Ingredients:
- 2 cups frozen prawns
- 4 cups dried pasta (I use penne for this recipe)
- 1 onion, finely chopped
- 5 garlic cloves, finely chopped
- ½ cup (4fl oz) dry white wine
- 1 tin chopped tomatoes
- 2 cups (24.5fl oz) chicken stock or water
- 1 cup (8fl oz) heavy cream

Method:
1. Drizzle some olive oil into your Instant Pot and keep the temperature at NORMAL.
2. Add the onions and garlic to the pot and sauté for a few minutes until the onions are soft.
3. Add the wine to the pot and simmer until the alcohol boils off.
4. Add the prawns, pasta, tomatoes, stock or water, salt, and pepper, stir to combine.
5. Secure the lid onto the pot and press the MANUAL button, adjust the temperature to HIGH, and adjust the time to 8 minutes.
6. Once the pot beeps, quick-release the pressure and remove the lid.
7. Stir the cream through the pasta before serving hot!

Crabmeat Macaroni

Crabmeat turns macaroni into a luxurious and special dish, without compromising the comfort food appeal. You could substitute the cheddar and mozzarella used in this recipe for your favorite cheeses!

Serves: 6-8
Time: approximately 30 minutes

Ingredients:
- 3 tbsp butter
- 1 tbsp plain flour
- 3 cups (24.5fl oz) milk
- ¼ tsp mustard powder (optional)
- 1 1/2 cups grated cheddar
- 1 cup grated mozzarella
- 5 cups dried macaroni
- 2 cups shredded crabmeat
- Fresh parsley, finely chopped

Method:
1. Cook the macaroni according to the packet instructions.
2. Press the SAUTE button on your Instant Pot and keep the temperature at NORMAL.
3. Add the butter to the pot and heat until melted.
4. Stir the flour into the pot to create a roux (flour and butter paste).
5. Whisk the milk and mustard powder (if using) into the pot until smooth and the lumps disappear.
6. Whisk the cheddar and mozzarella into the sauce until melted and combined.
7. Stir the cooked macaroni and the crabmeat into the sauce.
8. Secure the lid onto the pot and press the MANUAL button, adjust the temperature to HIGH, and set the time for 5 minutes.
9. Once the pot beeps, quick-release the pressure and remove the lid, serve your macaroni hot, with a sprinkle of fresh parsley!

Fish Stew

Use any white fish for this beautiful, light stew. Serve with crusty French bread, butter, and your favorite white wine.

Serves: 6
Time: approximately 30 minutes

Ingredients:
- 3 fillets of fresh white fish, cut into large chunks
- 1 cup frozen prawns
- 12 mussels in shells
- 3 large potatoes, peeled and cubed
- 2 large carrots, peeled and chopped into chunks
- 1 onion, finely chopped
- 6 garlic cloves, finely chopped
- 5 cups (40fl oz) fish stock
- 1 tin chopped tomatoes
- 1 tsp chili powder

Method:
1. Drizzle some olive oil into the Instant Pot and keep the temperature at NORMAL.
2. Add the onion and garlic to the pot, sauté until the onions are soft.
3. Add the fish, prawns, mussels, potatoes, carrots, stock, tomatoes, chili powder, salt, and pepper to the pot, stir to combine.
4. Secure the lid onto the pot and press the MEAT/STEW button, adjust the time to 20 minutes.
5. Once the pot beeps, quick-release the pressure and remove the lid.
6. Serve the hot stew immediately!

Crumbed Fish with Homemade Tomato Sauce

White fish, crumbed with a mixture of breadcrumbs and parmesan, with a tangy and slightly spicy tomato sauce. Serve with some oven roasted potatoes and voila, healthy fish and chips!

Serves: 4 (add more fish fillets to the recipe if you're serving more people, the sauce makes enough for about 10 serves)
Time: approximately 30 minutes

Ingredients:
- 4 fillets of fresh white fish
- 1 cup breadcrumbs (use panko crumbs for extra crunch)
- ½ cup grated parmesan cheese (mix the grated cheese with the breadcrumbs on a plate)
- 1 egg, lightly beaten
- 2 tins chopped tomatoes
- 1 onion, finely chopped
- 4 garlic cloves, finely chopped
- 2 tbsp red wine vinegar
- 2 tsp brown sugar
- 1 tsp chili flakes

Method:
1. Drizzle some olive oil into the Instant Pot and press the SAUTE button, keep the temperature at NORMAL.
2. Add the onion and garlic and sauté until soft.
3. Add the tomatoes, red wine vinegar, sugar, chili flakes, salt and pepper, stir to combine.
4. Secure the lid onto the pot and press the SOUP button, and adjust the time to 20 minutes.
5. Once the pot beeps, quick-release the pressure and remove the lid, whiz the sauce with a handheld blender until smooth before spooning it into a bottle, bowl, or jar.
6. Rinse the Instant Pot inner pot out and put it back into the pot.
7. Prepare the fish by coating each fillet in the beaten egg, then coating in the breadcrumbs and cheese.
8. Drizzle some olive oil into the Instant Pot and press the SAUTE button, adjust the temperature to HIGH.
9. Once the oil is hot, fry the fish fillets for about 2 minutes on both sides, or until golden and crispy and just cooked all the way through.
10. Serve the fish with a big spoonful of your homemade tomato sauce!

Easy Steamed Fish with Lemon and Herb Infusion

You will have noticed that many of these seafood recipes feature lemons. That's because lemon and fish go together so well! This is an extremely simple recipe, calling on the lemon and fresh herbs to give fresh fish a new attitude. Serve with buttered boiled potatoes, and some freshly boiled peas.

Serves: 4
Time: approximately 10 minutes

Ingredients:
- 4 fresh fish fillets
- 1 lemon, sliced into 8 slices
- Fresh mint, parsley, basil, and thyme, finely chopped

Method:
1. Pour 2 cups of water into the Instant Pot and place the steaming basket into the pot.
2. Place each fish fillet on a square of baking paper, (cut the square large enough to wrap the fillet up) and sprinkle with salt and pepper.
3. Sprinkle each fish fillet with the mixed fresh herbs.
4. Place 2 lemon slices on top of each fish fillet and wrap the fish up in the baking paper like a parcel.
5. Place the parcels into the steaming basket and secure the lid onto the Instant Pot.
6. Press the STEAM button and adjust the time to 3 minutes.
7. Once the pot beeps, allow the pot to release the steam naturally before removing the lid.
8. Serve the fish in the parcel so your guests can unwrap it to find their yummy, lemony, herby fish!

Smoked Fish Pies

A creamy fish filling inside a pastry case, with mozzarella cheese sprinkled on top! These pies are incredibly satisfying, and are a great way to get more fish into your diet. If you don't have pie dishes, you can make 1 big pie and just cook it in the oven until golden and cooked through.

Serves: makes 6 pies or 1 large one
Time: approximately 1 hour

Ingredients:
- 1 onion, finely chopped
- 4 garlic cloves, finely chopped
- 2 cups flaked smoked fish
- 2 fresh white fish fillets, chopped into small pieces
- 2 tbsp plain flour
- 1 cup (8fl oz) heavy cream
- 1 cup (8fl oz) full-fat milk
- 1 cup grated mozzarella
- Store-bought puff pastry

Method:
1. Preheat the oven to 374 degrees Fahrenheit.
2. Drizzle some olive oil into the Instant Pot and press the SAUTE button, keep the temperature at NORMAL, add the onions and garlic to the pot and sauté until the onions are soft.
3. Stir the flour into the onions and garlic until a paste forms.
4. Add the smoked fish, fresh fish pieces, cream, milk, salt, and pepper, stir to combine.
5. Allow to simmer for about 10 minutes until thick.
6. Line the greased and floured pie tins or a large pie dish with puff pastry.
7. Fill the pastry case/s with fish filling mixture.
8. Sprinkle the tops with grated mozzarella and place into the preheated oven.
9. Cook for about 15 minutes or until the pastry is golden and the mozzarella has melted.
10. Leave to cool slightly before devouring!

Potato and Tinned Salmon Bake

Tinned fish such as salmon and tuna are often overlooked as their fresh counterparts are preferred. Don't underestimate the versatility and nutritious benefits of tinned fish! You can stock up on tuna and salmon and keep them in the cupboard for next time you need an easy meal. This recipe uses tinned salmon, potatoes, and some eggs to create a filling and healthy bake.

Serves: 6
Time: approximately 45 minutes

Ingredients:
- 1 onion, finely chopped
- 4 garlic cloves, finely chopped
- 5 large potatoes, peeled and chopped into chunks
- 3 eggs, lightly beaten
- 1 cup (8fl oz) milk
- 2 large tins of salmon (about 14oz), drained
- 1 cup grated cheddar

Method:
1. Preheat the oven to 374 degrees Fahrenheit.
2. Pour 2 cups of water into the Instant Pot and place the steaming basket into the pot.
3. Place the potatoes, onion, garlic, salt, and pepper into the basket and secure the lid onto the pot.
4. Press the STEAM button and adjust the time to 10 minutes.
5. Once the pot beeps, quick-release the pressure and remove the lid.
6. In a large oven-proof dish, place the steamed potatoes and onions, the tinned salmon, eggs, milk, and cheddar cheese, stir to combine and make sure the potatoes and salmon are coated in egg and milk.
7. Place the dish into the oven and bake for about 12 minutes until set.
8. Serve with a fresh salad!

Thai Green Fish Curry

You can find Thai green curry paste in any supermarket or Asian food store. Fish creates a light curry, where the flavors of the spices and coconut can really shine. Serve with rice of course!

Serves: 6
Time: approximately 35 minutes

Ingredients:
- 4 tbsp Thai green curry paste
- 1 onion, roughly chopped
- 4 fresh white fish fillets, chopped into chunks
- 2 tins full-fat coconut milk (about 32floz)
- 1 cup (8fl oz) fish stock
- 1 tsp sugar

Method:
1. Drizzle some olive oil into the Instant Pot and press the SAUTE button, keep the temperature at NORMAL.
2. Add the curry paste and onions to the pot and sauté until the onions are soft.
3. Add the fish, coconut milk, stock, and sugar to the pot, stir to combine.
4. Secure the lid onto the pot and press the MEAT/STEW button and adjust the time to 20 minutes.
5. Once the pot beeps, quick-release the pressure and remove the lid.
6. Serve while hot, on top of a pile of fluffy rice!

Prawn and Noodle Salad

Cold noodles with garlicy prawns: a perfect summer salad. Use any noodles you like, I like to use soba noodles, but because they might not be available in all supermarkets, I have used egg noodles in this recipe.

Serves: 6
Time: approximately 25 minutes

Ingredients:
- 3 cups frozen prawns
- 28 oz dried egg noodles (or any other noodles such as ramen, rice, or soba)
- 1 green onion (scallion), white part sliced
- 2 garlic cloves, crushed
- 1 tsp sesame oil
- 1 lime

Method:
1. Prepare the noodles according to the packet instructions, then run them under cold water until cold. Drain and set aside.
2. Drizzle some olive oil into your Instant Pot and press the SAUTE button, keep the temperature at NORMAL.
3. Once the pot is hot, add the garlic and prawns and sauté until cooked through.
4. Place the noodles into a large salad bowl and add the garlic prawns, green onion, sesame oil, juice of one lime, salt, and pepper, stir to combine and coat the noodles.
5. Enjoy immediately!

Garlic Butter Calamari

Put out a platter of these garlic butter calamari rings at your next dinner party or barbeque, and they will be devoured! You can make an easy dipping sauce by mixing sweet chilli sauce with sour cream and lemon juice.

Serves: about 8 as a snack or starter
Time: approximately 12 minutes

Ingredients:
- 2 lb calamari, cleaned
- 3 tbsp butter
- 6 garlic cloves, crushed
- 2 tsp finely chopped fresh chives (optional)

Method:
1. Press the SAUTE button on your Instant Pot and adjust the temperature to HIGH.
2. Place the butter and garlic into the pot and heat until the butter is melted.
3. Add the calamari to the pot with a sprinkle of salt and pepper, stir to coat in garlic butter.
4. Sauté the calamari until cooked through but not overcooked and rubbery (have a taste, you'll know when they're ready!).
5. Pile the calamari onto a platter or into a serving bowl and enjoy!

Fish Burger Patties

I like to eat my fish burgers with beetroot slices, tomato, lettuce, and a generous dollop of garlic aioli. You can fill your burgers with whatever you like! These fish patties are simple and tasty, and can be made with any type of fresh white fish.

Serves: makes about 12 patties
Time: approximately 15 minutes

Ingredients:
- 2 lb fresh white fish fillets
- 1 onion, finely chopped
- 5 garlic cloves, finely chopped
- 2 eggs, lightly beaten
- 1 cup bread crumbs
- 1 tsp ground paprika
- 1 tsp chili powder
- 1 tsp ground cumin

Method:
1. Pour 2 cups of water into the Instant Pot and place the steaming basket into the pot.
2. Place the fish fillets into the steaming basket (you may have to do 2 batches if there's a lot of fish).
3. Secure the lid onto the pot and press the STEAM button, adjust the time to 3 minutes.
4. Once the pot beeps, quick-release the pressure and remove the fish from the basket and place into a large bowl.
5. Tip any leftover water out of the Instant Pot and drizzle it with olive oil to get ready for frying.
6. With 2 forks, flake the cooked fish in the bowl you placed it in.
7. Add the onions, garlic, eggs, breadcrumbs, paprika, chili, cumin, salt, and pepper to the bowl, stir to thoroughly combine.
8. Press the SAUTE button on your Instant Pot and keep the temperature at NORMAL.
9. Form the patty mixture into large patties (or however large or small you wish!) and drop them into the hot oil, fry on both sides until both sides are golden brown.
10. Assemble your fish burgers and have a feast!

Vegan & Vegetarian

This collection of vegetarian (V) and vegan (VG) recipes caters to different tastes and cuisines. There's a bit of Italian, some Asian fusion, and a take on the classic burger. Feel free to adjust and modify these recipes to suit your tastes and dietary requirements.

Butternut pumpkin and carrot soup (V, VG)

Butternut pumpkin are great friends when it comes to soup. I use coconut cream to finish this soup, as it gives a creamy flavor and texture without using dairy.

Serves: 6
Time: approximately 35 minutes

Ingredients:
- 1 butternut pumpkin (squash), skin and seeds removed, flesh cut into chunks
- 5 large carrots, chopped into chunks (no need to peel)
- 2 onions, finely chopped
- 8 garlic cloves, finely chopped
- 4 cups (32fl oz) vegetable stock
- 1 can coconut cream

Method:
1. Place the butternut, carrots, onions, garlic, stock, salt, and pepper into the Instant Pot.
2. Secure the lid onto the pot and press the SOUP button, adjust the time to 40 minutes.
3. Once the pot beeps, quick-release the pressure and remove the lid.
4. Give the soup a stir before whizzing it to a smooth consistency with a handheld stick blender.
5. Stir the coconut cream into the soup, if it's too thick, simply add some extra water or vegetable stock!

Veggie-packed fried rice (V, VG)

This fried rice is Vegan and Vegetarian friendly, so it doesn't have any eggs. But if you're an egg-eating vegetarian, feel free to add an egg in place of the tofu! This is where frozen veggies come in very, very handy indeed. However, if you don't have frozen, just use fresh.

Serves: 6
Time: approximately 30 minutes

Ingredients:
- 2 cups dry basmati rice (or brown rice, if you prefer the nuttier flavor)
- 2 cups frozen mixed veggies (carrots, peas, and corn)
- 1 onion, finely chopped
- 1 block firm tofu (about 14 oz), cut into small chunks
- 4 garlic cloves, finely chopped
- 1 tbsp grated fresh ginger
- 3 tbsp soy sauce
- 1 tsp sesame oil

Method:
1. Cook the rice in your Instant Pot according to which type of rice you are using.
2. Once the rice has cooked, remove it from the pot and set aside, was the inner pot and put it back so you can carry on with the recipe.
3. Drizzle some olive oil into the Instant Pot and press the SAUTE button, keep the temperature at normal.
4. Add the onions, garlic, and ginger to the pot, sauté until soft.
5. Add the frozen veggies and sauté until cooked through.
6. Add the tofu to the pot and sauté, while stirring, until starting to turn golden.
7. Add the cooked rice to the pot and keep stirring while it cooks.
8. Pour the soy sauce and sesame oil into the pot and stir to combine and coat the rice, tofu, and veggies.
9. Serve with a side of bean sprouts and some peanuts!

Instant Pot Spaghetti Bolognese (V, VG)

This Bolognese is made with lentils instead of minced meat! The high fiber content makes this dish a healthy and nutritious option for everyone.

Serves: 6
Time: approximately 40 minutes

Ingredients:
- 2 tins brown lentils (about 3 cups of lentils once drained)
- 1 onion, finely chopped
- 6 garlic cloves, finely chopped
- ½ cup red wine
- 2 tins chopped tomatoes
- 1 tsp sugar
- 1 tsp mixed dried herbs
- Enough spaghetti for 6 people (roughly about 18 oz)

Method:
1. Drizzle some olive oil into your Instant Pot and press the SAUTE button, keep the temperature at NORMAL.
2. Add the onions and garlic to the pot and sauté until soft.
3. Add the red wine to the pot and simmer for a few minutes to boil off the alcohol.
4. Add the lentils, tomatoes, sugar, herbs, salt, and pepper to the pot and stir to combine.
5. Secure the lid onto the pot and press the BEAN/CHILLI button, adjust the time to 25 minutes.
6. Once the pot beeps, quick-release the pressure and remove the lid.
7. Cook your spaghetti in a large pot of boiling, salted water as the Bolognese cooks.
8. Serve with a drizzle of olive oil!

3-Bean Chili (V, VG)

3-bean chili features black beans, red kidney beans, and cannellini beans. Tomatoes, spices, and lots of garlic infuse the beans to create a thick, warming, and versatile chili to use as the base of many vegan and vegetarian dishes.

Serves: 6-8
Time: approximately 30 minutes

Ingredients:
- 2 onions, roughly chopped
- 8 garlic cloves, roughly chopped
- 2 tins black beans, drained
- 2 tins red kidney beans, drained
- 1 tin cannellini beans, drained
- 2 tins chopped tomatoes
- 1 tsp ground paprika
- 2 tsp ground chili
- 1 tsp ground coriander
- 1 tsp ground cumin
- 1 tsp sugar (optional)

Method:
1. Place the onions, garlic, black, red kidney, and cannellini beans, tomatoes, chili, coriander, cumin, sugar, salt and pepper into the Instant Pot (yup, that's all of the ingredients!) and add 1 cup of water, stir to combine.
2. Secure the lid onto the pot and press the BEAN/CHILI button, keep the time to the default 30 minutes.
3. Once the pot beeps, quick-release the pressure and remove the lid.
4. Stir the chili and serve while hot, with a side of corn chips and a big dollop of guacamole...just a suggestion!

Coconut Rice with Garlic, Ginger, Fresh Chili (V, VG)

Coconut rice is one of those things that I just can't leave alone...as soon as I serve it up I have to put the leftovers straight into the fridge so I'm not tempted to go back for more servings! This recipe features garlic, rice and red chili. It can be served as a side, or as the main dish on lazy nights, with some steamed broccoli.

Serves: 6 as a main dish
Time: approximately 15 minutes

Ingredients:
- 3 cups dry basmati rice
- 2 cups (16fl oz) coconut milk
- 2 cups (16fl oz) vegetable stock
- 5 garlic cloves, crushed
- 2 tbsp grated fresh ginger
- 1 fresh red chili, finely chopped

Method:
1. Place the rice, coconut milk, stock, garlic, ginger, chili, salt, and pepper to the Instant Pot, and stir to combine.
2. Secure the lid onto the pot and press the RICE button, allow the rice to cook automatically.
3. Once the pot beeps, allow the pressure to release naturally before removing the lid.
4. Serve your coconut rice with a drizzle of soy sauce!

Mushrooms Burgers (V)

These burgers are not vegan, as they feature eggs a good hunk of cheese! However, you can substitute for vegan eggs and cheese if you like. If you are following the Keto diet or you're simply trying to avoid carbs at night, you could use lettuce instead of buns.

Serves: 6
Time: approximately 25 minutes

Ingredients:
- 6 large Portobello mushrooms
- 2 eggs, lightly beaten
- ¾ cup grated parmesan cheese
- ¾ breadcrumbs
- 6 burger buns
- 1 large tomato, sliced into 6 slices
- Iceberg lettuce
- Mayonnaise (for assembling the burgers)
- Pickles (optional)

Method:
1. Combine the grated parmesan and the breadcrumbs on a plate.
2. Dip the mushrooms into the beaten egg, then into the parmesan and breadcrumbs to coat them thoroughly.
3. Drizzle some olive oil into the Instant Pot and press the SAUTE button, keep the temperature at NORMAL.
4. Fry the mushrooms on both sides until golden and crispy.
5. Assemble the burgers by layering tomatoes, lettuce, mayo, pickles, and the mushroom patty (or however you like! I'm not going to tell you how to make a burger!).

Teriyaki Tofu Rice Paper Rolls (V, VG)

Rice paper can be found in most supermarkets and all Asian food stores. These rolls are filled with teriyaki tofu, avocado, carrot, and lettuce. A simple dipping sauce can be made of soy sauce, sesame oil, and lime juice.

Serves: makes 12 rolls (about 3 rolls per person)
Time: approximately 25 minutes

Ingredients:
- 12 round rice paper sheets
- 1 block firm tofu (about 14oz), cut into 12 strips
- 1 large avocado, stone removed, flesh sliced
- 1 carrot, peeled and cut into strips
- 1/3 head of iceberg lettuce, shredded
- 1/3 cup soy sauce
- 3 tbsp honey
- 1 tbsp grated fresh ginger
- 2 garlic cloves, crushed

Method:
1. In a small bowl, mix together the soy sauce, honey, ginger, and garlic cloves.
2. Add the tofu to the bowl and make sure all of the pieces are coated in sauce.
3. Press the SAUTE button on your Instant Pot and adjust the temperature to HIGH, drizzle some olive or sesame oil into the pot.
4. Once the pot is hot, place the tofu and sauce into the pot and fry on all sides until just starting to caramelize.
5. Get a large board ready with your carrot, lettuce, tofu, and avocado ready.
6. Place a damp tea towel on a plate, so you can place the filled rolls there to keep them from drying out.
7. Submerge the rice paper sheets in warm water until they are soft, lay them on the board and place the fillings in a line along the center.
8. Wrap the rolls up and fold the ends in.
9. Serve them right away, with a dipping sauce of your choice!

Vegetarian Lasagna (V)

Sometimes I think I like vegetarian lasagna better than "meaty" lasagna. The pumpkin, spinach, mushrooms, and capsicum offer so much texture and flavor! Don't be alarmed at the long list of ingredients, they're all standard and easy to find if you don't already have them hanging about in your kitchen. There are lots of different cooking options in this recipe. You can cook all of the components in the Instant Pot, or you can utilize the oven and the stove to cook lots of components at the same time.

Serves: 6-8
Time: approximately 1 hour and 10 minutes

Ingredients:
- 1 onion, finely chopped
- 6 garlic cloves, finely chopped
- 2 tins chopped tomatoes
- ½ cup red wine
- 1 tsp brown sugar
- 1 tsp chili flakes
- 6 large lasagna sheets (get the ones you don't need to pre-boil!)
- 2 cups cubed pumpkin, (skin removed, about ¼ of a pumpkin)
- 2 red capsicums, core and seeds removed, sliced
- 2 cups sliced mushrooms
- 4 cups baby spinach leaves
- 3 tbsp butter
- 2 tbsp plain flour
- 4 cups (32fl oz) milk
- 2 cups grated mozzarella

Method:
1. Make the white sauce by getting a small pot ready on the stove, add the butter to the pot and heat it gently until melted, whisk the flour into the butter until a paste forms, whisk the milk into the paste and keep whisking as it thickens, season with salt and pepper. Once the sauce is thick, set it to one side.
2. You can either roast the pumpkin in the oven at 374 degrees Fahrenheit until soft and golden, or you can STEAM it in the Instant Pot by pouring 2 cups of water into the pot and placing the pumpkin into the steaming basket, steam for 10 minutes.

3. Make the tomato sauce by drizzling some olive oil into the Instant Pot, press the SAUTE button and keep the temperature at NORMAL.
4. Add the onion and garlic to the pot and sauté until soft, add the wine and simmer until the aroma of alcohol has disappeared.
5. Add the sugar, chilli flakes, tinned tomatoes, salt, and pepper, simmer for about 12 minutes until thick and reduced.
6. Either in the Instant Pot or a frying pan, SAUTE the mushrooms, capsicum, and spinach until the spinach has wilted and the other veggies are cooked through.
7. Assemble the lasagna by spreading a spoonful of tomato sauce into the bottom of a large rectangular glass dish, place a layer of spinach, capsicum and mushrooms on top, lay down a lasagna sheet, spread a layer of tomato sauce over the sheet and drizzle some white sauce over, lightly mash the pumpkin and place it in one layer, keep layering the ingredients until they are all gone.
8. Finish with a layer of white sauce, then sprinkle the grated cheese over the top.
9. Bake in the oven at 374 degrees Fahrenheit for about 30 minutes.

Pumpkin, Carrot, and Peanut Salad (V, VG)

This salad is full of golden colors and lovely textures. It's a great accompaniment to picnics and Summer dinner tables, or it can be enjoyed as a light main dish. I use salted, roasted peanuts, but cashews would also work!

Serves: 6
Time: approximately 25 minutes

Ingredients:
- 1 small pumpkin, peeled, seeds removed, and flesh chopped into cubes (about 5 cups)
- 4 carrots, peeled and chopped into rounds
- 1 cup roasted and salted peanuts
- Large handful of fresh mint, finely chopped
- 2 spring onions (scallions), white part finely chopped

Method:
1. Pour 2 cups of water into the Instant Pot and place the steaming basket into the pot.
2. Place the pumpkin and carrot into the basket, sprinkle with salt and pepper.
3. Secure the lid onto the pot and press the STEAM button, keep the time to the default 10 minutes.
4. Once the pot beeps, quick-release the pressure and remove the lid.
5. Take the basket of veggies out of the pot and remove any excess liquid from the inner pot.
6. Drizzle some olive oil into the pot and press the SAUTE button, keep the temperature at NORMAL.
7. Add the cooked pumpkin and carrot to the pot and sauté until golden and starting to caramelize.
8. Place the double-cooked veggies in a large salad bowl and add the peanuts, mint, spring onions, and a drizzle of olive oil, stir to combine.
9. Serve warm or cold!

Vegetarian Laksa (V, VG)

Laksa is a thin soup of coconut milk and curry paste, with veggies, tofu, and udon noodles. You can substitute the veggies in this recipe for any other veggie you like! You can find laksa paste at most supermarkets, and all Asian food stores. Use red curry paste if you can't find laksa paste.

Serves: 6
Time: approximately 15 minutes

Ingredients:
- 3 tbsp laksa paste
- 2 tins coconut milk
- 1 cup (8fl oz) vegetable stock
- 1 cup sliced mushrooms
- 1 cup sliced carrots
- ½ broccoli, cut into florets
- 1 block tofu, (about 14 oz), cut into small chunks
- 22 oz udon noodles

Method:
1. Press the SAUTE button on your Instant Pot and keep the temperature at NORMAL.
2. Add the laksa paste to the pot and sauté for about 1 minute until fragrant
3. Add the coconut milk, stock, mushrooms, carrots, broccoli, tofu, and udon noodles to the pot.
4. Secure the lid onto the pot and press the MANUAL button, adjust the temperature to HIGH, and adjust the temperature to 4 minutes.
5. Once the pot beeps, quick-release the pressure and remove the lid.
6. Serve the laksa with a squeeze of lime and some fresh coriander!

Breakfast

Breakfast doesn't need to be a boring bowl of cereal with some milk! The Instant Pot opens up the possibilities for amazing breakfasts all week round. Some of these recipes are a bit naughtier than others, and are best for special weekends with loved ones.

Cinnamon and Stone Fruit Oatmeal

Oatmeal is so easy and fast to create in the Instant Pot, and this recipe features stone fruits and cinnamon. You can use any stone fruits, but my favorites are plums and peaches!

Serves: 4
Time: approximately 10 minutes

Ingredients:
- 2 cups wholegrain oats
- 1 cup (8fl oz) full-fat milk
- Pinch of salt
- 1 tsp cinnamon
- 2 peaches, stones removed, flesh cut into chunks
- 2 plums, stones removed, flesh cut into chunks

Method:
1. Place the oats, milk, cinnamon, salt, peaches, plums, and 3 cups of water into the Instant Pot.
2. Secure the lid onto the pot and press the MANUAL button, adjust the temperature to HIGH, and adjust the time to 6 minutes.
3. Once the pot beeps, quick-release the pressure and remove the lid.
4. Stir the oatmeal before serving piping hot, with a splash of cold milk and some honey!

Breakfast Burritos

Breakfast burritos can be filled with so many different fillings, but these ones feature eggs, black beans, cheese, and tomato (classics!). Serve with some slices of fresh avocado and a hot coffee...mmm what a way to start the day.

Serves: 4
Time: approximately 30 minutes

Ingredients:
- 4 round tortilla wraps
- 5 eggs, lightly beaten
- 1 tin black beans, drained
- ½ cup grated cheddar cheese
- 1 large tomato, chopped into chunks
- 1 handful fresh coriander, roughly chopped

Method:
1. Press the SAUTE button on your Instant Pot and adjust the temperature to LOW, drizzle some olive oil into the pot.
2. Add the eggs to the pot and gently push them with a flat wooden spoon as they cook, until they are very lightly scrambled.
3. Push the eggs to one side of the pot and add the black beans to the pot, sauté the beans for a minute or two until hot and slightly mushy.
4. Place the tortilla wraps on the bench and fill each one with equal amounts of scrambled egg and hot black beans.
5. Place some chopped tomatoes and some grated cheese on top of the eggs and beans.
6. Sprinkle with coriander.
7. Roll the burritos up tightly and lay them in a greased heatproof dish (make sure it fits in the Instant Pot!).
8. Sprinkle the rolled burritos with more cheese then cover the dish with foil.
9. Pour 1 cup of water into the Instant Pot and place a trivet into the pot, place the dish on top of the trivet and secure the lid onto the pot, press the MANUAL button and adjust the temperature to HIGH, adjust the time for 12 minutes.
10. Once the pot beeps, quick-release the pressure, remove the lid, and serve the hot, melty burritos immediately!

Breakfast Sweet Potato Frittata

Frittatas are usually made with regular potatoes, but I think the sweetness and softness of sweet potatoes makes for a lovely change. The bacon can be swapped for chorizo or salmon! Serve with fresh tomato relish and of course...HOT COFFEE.

Serves: 4-6
Time: approximately 20 minutes

Ingredients:
- 2 large sweet potatoes, washed and cut into small chunks
- 5 eggs, lightly beaten
- 5 rashers of streaky bacon, cut into small pieces
- Large handful of fresh parsley, finely chopped
- ½ cup grated cheddar cheese

Method:
1. Pour 2 cups of water into the Instant Pot and place the steaming basket into the pot.
2. Place the sweet potatoes into the pot and secure the lid, press the STEAM button, and adjust the time to 3 minutes.
3. Once the pot beeps, quick-release the steam and remove the lid, take the sweet potatoes out of the pot and discard any leftover water from the pot.
4. Drizzle some olive oil into the pot and spread it around so it fully coats the bottom of the pot, press the SAUTE button and adjust the temperature to LOW.
5. Add the bacon to the pot and sauté for a couple of minutes until sizzling and cooked.
6. Add the steamed sweet potatoes to the pot and stir to combine with the bacon, spread them out to coat the bottom of the pot.
7. Pour the beaten eggs over the sweet potatoes and spread out to cover the potatoes, sprinkle the cheese over the top.
8. Leave to gently cook for about 10 minutes or until the eggs have set.
9. Sprinkle the parsley over the frittata before serving!

Slow-Cooked Apple Whole Oats

Get these oats slow cooking before you go to bed and wake up to beautiful, soft, and apple-infused whole oatmeal. Use any type of apples you have.

Serves: 4-6
Time: approximately 8 hours

Ingredients:
- 3 cups whole oats
- 2 cups (16fl oz) full-fat milk
- 1 tsp ground cinnamon
- 3 apples, peeled, cored, and cut into chunks
- Pinch of salt

Method:
1. Place the oats, milk, cinnamon, apples, salt, and 4 cups of water into the Instant Pot, stir to combine.
2. Secure the lid onto the pot and press the SLOW COOK button, adjust the temperature to LOW, and adjust the time to 8 hours.
3. Make sure the steam valve is open.
4. In the morning, remove the lid, stir the oatmeal, and serve immediately!

Big breakfast fry

When you've got some friends over in the morning, maybe after a big night out, cook them this Big Breakfast Fry! Hash browns, eggs, bacon, tomatoes, and beans...not for light eaters!

Serves: 5
Time: approximately 30 minutes

Ingredients:
- 5 frozen hash browns
- 6 eggs
- 10 rashers of streaky bacon
- 3 large tomatoes, cut in half and sprinkled with salt and pepper
- 1 tin baked beans

Method:
1. Drizzle some olive oil into the Instant Pot and press the SAUTE button, adjust the temperature to HIGH.
2. Once the pot is hot, lay the hash browns in one layer on the bottom of the pot, fry for a couple of minutes on both sides until golden, crispy, and cooked through.
3. Remove the hash browns from the pot and set aside.
4. Add the bacon to one side of the pot, and place the tomatoes cut-side down on the other side of the pot, sauté for a few minutes until the bacon is crispy on both sides, and the tomatoes are starting to caramelize and soften, remove from the pot.
5. Cook the eggs however you and your guests prefer, it's easy to scramble eggs in the Instant Pot so that would be my choice!
6. Heat the baked beans in the microwave on high for about 2 minutes.
7. Add the tomatoes, bacon, hash browns, and scrambled eggs (if applicable) back into the Instant Pot to heat up and become extra crispy for a few minutes, don't worry if they start to meld together, that's good!
8. Serve with fresh avocado, orange juice, and a squeeze of tomato ketchup!

Naughty French Toast with Berries

I call this "naughty" French Toast because it features chocolate chips and cinnamon sugar. If you can find brioche buns at your local supermarket or bakery, pick some up! They make a lovely French toast. Otherwise, just use any thick white bread you can find.

Serves: 4
Time: approximately 30 minutes

Ingredients:
- Large knob of butter
- 8 slices of thick white bread or brioche (a day or two old is okay!)
- 4 eggs, lightly beaten
- 2 tbsp milk
- ½ cup chocolate chips (dark or milk)
- 1 tsp cinnamon
- 2 tbsp sugar
- 2 cups frozen berries

Method:
1. Get the Instant Pot ready by pressing the SAUTE button and keeping the temperature to NORMAL.
2. Place a knob of butter into the pot to melt.
3. Mix the cinnamon and sugar together on a plate.
4. Dip the bread or brioche into the beaten eggs and thoroughly coat.
5. Transfer to the plate of cinnamon sugar and coat on both sides.
6. Place the coated toast into the hot melted butter in the Instant Pot and fry on both sides.
7. Once both sides have been fried, sprinkle some chocolate chips on top of each piece of toast and leave for about 1 minute until the chocolate begins to soften and melt.
8. Remove the toasts from the pot and place on serving plates.
9. Add the frozen berries to the pot with ½ cup of water and stir, allow the berries to come to a simmer until they form a thick sauce.
10. Spoon the hot berries over the French toast before serving!

Spinach, Feta, and Mushroom Breakfast Side

This dish is lovely when served on the side of eggs on toast, or frittatas. It adds an extra boost of veggie goodness and the feta gives a hit of salty creaminess.

Serves: 6 as a side
Time: approximately 10 minutes

Ingredients:
- 4 cups baby spinach leaves
- 7 oz feta cheese, crumbled
- 2 cups sliced mushrooms (any type, button mushrooms work well!)
- 2 garlic cloves, finely chopped
- ½ tsp dried mixed herbs

Method:
1. Drizzle some olive oil into your Instant Pot and press the SAUTE button, keep the temperature at NORMAL.
2. Add the garlic to the pot and heat for about 30 seconds until soft but not burnt.
3. Add the spinach, mushrooms, herbs, salt, and pepper, sauté until the spinach has wilted and the mushrooms are soft.
4. Add the feta cheese and stir gently to combine.
5. Place into a serving dish and eat hot or warm!

TIP: you can also use this mixture as a mini pie filling for appetizers and starters!

Potato and Zucchini Cakes

Sometimes I use these potato and zucchini cakes as a replacement for bread when I feel like eggs on toast. The outsides become gloriously golden and crispy, and the insides remain soft and tender.

Serves: makes about 12 cakes (3 per serving)
Time: approximately 20 minutes

Ingredients:
- 4 large potatoes, peeled and grated (the grater attachment on a food processor makes the job easy!)
- 2 large zucchinis, grated and squeezed in a tea towel to remove excess moisture
- 2 eggs, lightly beaten
- ½ tsp chilli powder
- Knob of butter, for frying

Method:
1. In a large bowl, combine the grated potatoes, zucchinis, eggs, chilli powder, salt, and pepper.
2. Press the SAUTE button on your Instant Pot and keep the temperature at NORMAL.
3. Drizzle some olive oil into the pot and add the knob of butter.
4. Once the butter has melted and the oil is hot, place large dollops of mixture into the pot and fry on both sides for a couple of minutes each, until golden and crispy.
5. Place the cakes on a plate lined with paper towels as they come out of the pot.
6. Serve the cooked cakes with poached eggs and bacon!

Banana Coconut Pancakes

These pancakes are surprisingly healthy...until you add lots of cream and maple syrup! Or, for a healthier option, Greek yoghurt and honey. A few chopped strawberries on top never goes astray.

Serves: makes about 10 small pancakes
Time: approximately 20 minutes

Ingredients:
- 2 large bananas, mashed
- 1 cup desiccated coconut
- 2 eggs, lightly beaten
- ½ cup almond milk (or any kind of milk you have)
- ½ cup almond meal
- 1 tsp ground cinnamon
- 1 tsp baking powder

Method:
1. In a large bowl, combine the bananas, coconut, eggs, milk, almond meal cinnamon, baking powder, and a pinch of salt.
2. Drizzle some coconut oil into the Instant Pot (or use butter instead) and press the SAUTE button, keep the temperature at NORMAL.
3. Drop large spoonsful of mixture into the hot pot and fry on both sides for a couple of minutes until bubbling and golden.
4. Serve with Greek yoghurt, honey, and berries (that's just a suggestion, top with anything you fancy!).

Banana Blueberry Bread

Banana bread can be made in the Instant Pot! I've put this recipe in the Breakfast section because I think banana bread is such a special treat when eaten warm, with butter on top, at breakfast time. I've added blueberries to this recipe, but you could use any frozen berries.

Serves: makes 1 banana bread, about 10 slices
Time: approximately 1 hour

Ingredients:
- 3 very brown bananas, mashed
- 2 eggs, lightly beaten
- ½ cup (4fl oz) rice bran oil, coconut oil, or sunflower oil
- ½ cup packed brown sugar
- 2 cups plain flour
- 1 tsp baking powder
- ½ tsp baking soda
- 1 tsp cinnamon
- 1 cup frozen raspberries

Method:
1. In a large bowl, add the bananas, eggs, oil, and sugar, whisk to combine.
2. Add the flour, baking powder, baking soda, and cinnamon to the bowl, stir to combine.
3. Fold the blueberries into the mixture.
4. Pour the mixture into a butter-greased (or lined with baking paper) loaf tin and cover the top with foil (ensure the tin fits in the Instant Pot first).
5. Pour 1 cup of water into the Instant Pot and place a trivet into the pot.
6. Place the loaf tin on top of the trivet and secure the lid onto the pot.
7. Press the MANUAL button, adjust the temperature to HIGH, and adjust the time to 35 minutes.
8. Once the pot beeps, allow the pressure to release naturally before removing the lid and taking the banana bread out of the pot.
9. Leave to cool for about 5 minutes before turning out onto a board and slicing.

Slow Cooked Baked Beans

Baked beans don't have to come from a can, in fact, homemade is even more delicious. These baked beans are slow cooked to truly infuse and enrich the flavors. You do need to soak the dried beans overnight, so be prepared to wait a while before you get to enjoy your beans, the wait is worth it though!

Serves: 6-8
Time: overnight plus 10 hours

Ingredients:
- 4 cups dried navy beans
- 1 ½ cups tomato passata or puree
- 2 onions, finely chopped
- ¾ cup packed brown sugar
- 2 tbsp red wine vinegar

Method:
1. Soak the dried beans overnight, drain the water when you're ready to make the baked beans.
2. Place the beans, tomato passata, onions, brown sugar, red wine vinegar, salt, and pepper into the Instant Pot, stir to combine.
3. Secure the lid onto the pot and press the SLOW COOK button, adjust the temperature to LOW, and adjust the time to 10 hours.
4. Make sure the steam valve is open.
5. Once the pot beeps, quick-release the steam and remove the lid.
6. Stir the beans and serve hot with a slice of buttered toast!

Soft-boiled eggs

Soft boiled eggs can be eaten in a sandwich (smash them between fresh, crusty bread, and sprinkle with salt and pepper), or eat with toast batons and bacon. Buy free range eggs if you can!

Serves: makes 4 eggs but you can add more
Time: approximately 7 minutes

Ingredients:

4 eggs

Method:

1. Pour 2 cups of water into the Instant Pot and place the steaming basket into the pot.
2. Place the eggs into the steaming basket and secure the lid onto the pot.
3. Press the MANUAL button, adjust the temperature to LOW, and adjust the time to 4 minutes.
4. Once the pot beeps, quick-release the pressure and remove the lid.
5. Take the eggs out and eat how you please!

Instant Pot Breakfast Quiche

This quiche features asparagus and spinach, which makes it a great way to add more veggies to your diet. If asparagus is not in season but you still want to make this quiche, you could substitute for zucchini, or simply add more spinach.

Serves: 4-6
Time: approximately 40 minutes

Ingredients:
- Store-bought puff pastry
- 6 eggs, lightly beaten
- 2 cups baby spinach leaves
- 10 asparagus spears, woody ends cut off
- ½ cup grated cheddar cheese
- 6 rashers of streaky bacon

Method:
1. Preheat the oven to 374 degrees Fahrenheit and prepare a pie dish by greasing it with butter and sprinkling with flour.
2. Pour 2 cups of water into the Instant Pot and place the steaming basket into the pot.
3. Place the asparagus into the basket and place the spinach leaves on top of the asparagus, sprinkle with salt.
4. Secure the lid onto the pot and press the STEAM button, adjust the time to 3 minutes.
5. Once the pot beeps, quick-release the pressure and remove the lid, take the veggies out and leave to one side.
6. Line your greased pie dish with pastry and prick it with a fork (to let the steam out as it bakes) and place into the preheated oven for 10 minutes until the pastry starts to turn golden.
7. Take the pastry-lined dish from the oven and pour in the beaten eggs, spread the cooked spinach over the eggs, lay the cooked asparagus in a line over the spinach, sprinkle the cheese over the asparagus, lay the bacon over the cheese.
8. Place the quiche back into the oven and cook for about 12 minutes or until the bacon is cooked and the cheese is bubbling beneath!

Breakfast fruit crumble

I love fruit crumble so much I had to find a way to eat it for breakfast without compromising my (mostly) healthy diet! Serve with Greek yoghurt and enjoy.

Serves: 6
Time: approximately 45 minutes

Ingredients:
- 5 apples, peeled, cored, and sliced
- 1 peach or nectarine, stone removed, sliced
- 1 cup frozen mixed berries
- 1 cup almond flour
- ½ cup desiccated coconut
- ½ cup flaked almonds
- ½ cup coconut oil, heated in the microwave
- ½ cup honey
- 1 tsp cinnamon

Method:
1. In a medium-sized bowl, add the almond flour, coconut, flaked almonds, coconut oil, honey, and cinnamon, stir to combine until a soft, crumbly texture forms.
2. In a heatproof dish (make sure it fits into the Instant Pot) layer the apples, peach/nectarine, and berries.
3. Pour a few tablespoons of water over the fruit.
4. Sprinkle the crumble over top of the fruit and cover the dish with tin foil.
5. Pour 1 cup of water into the Instant Pot and place a trivet into the pot.
6. Place the crumble onto the trivet and secure the lid onto the pot.
7. Press the BEAN/CHILI button and adjust the time to 25 minutes.
8. Once the pot beeps, quick-release the pressure and remove the lid.
9. Take the crumble out of the pot and leave to cool slightly before serving!

TIP: this crumble is just as good (if not better) eaten cold.

Salmon Bites for Champagne Breakfasts

Salmon and cream cheese belong on the menu for ALL champagne breakfasts and morning celebrations. You'll need some mini muffin cases, but they're pretty easy to find.

Serves: makes about 20 bites
Time: approximately 20 minutes

Ingredients:
- 1 block (about 17 oz) plain cream cheese
- 1 packet smoked salmon strips (about 4 oz)
- 5 eggs, lightly beaten
- Fresh chives, finely chopped

Method:
1. Lay the mini muffin cases onto a rack which can fit into the instant pot (the one which came with the pot is ideal!).
2. Fill each case with a small amount of beaten egg.
3. Place a heaped teaspoonful of cream cheese into each case.
4. Place a small amount of smoked salmon on top of the cream cheese.
5. Sprinkle the cases with chives.
6. Pour 1 cup of water into the Instant Pot.
7. Carefully place the rack into the pot without spilling the egg out of the cases!
8. Secure the lid onto the pot and press the MANUAL button, adjust the temperature to LOW and adjust the time to 10 minutes.
9. Once the pot beeps, quick-release the pressure before removing the lid.
10. Very carefully remove the salmon bites and place on a platter to cool before serving.

Appetizers

These small bites of flavor and texture will wow and satisfy your guests next time you host a party, or are required to "bring a plate" to a dinner or cocktail party. Some of these recipes can be made for light dinners and daytime snacks too.

Spinach and Feta Puffs

The "puff" comes from a small amount of baking powder added to the mixture. I guess you could describe them as tiny spinach and feta muffins. You could even take them up a notch by adding a dollop of cream cheese inside for a special surprise.

Serves: makes about 20 puffs
Time: approximately 20 minutes

Ingredients:
- 4 eggs, lightly beaten
- 1 ½ cup plain flour
- ½ tsp baking powder
- 4 cups baby spinach leaves, cooked on high in the microwave for 3 minutes with a tablespoon of water
- 7 oz feta cheese, crumbled
- ½ cup grated mozzarella

Method:
1. Once you have cooked the spinach in the microwave, place it on a board and finely chop it.
2. In a large bowl, add the eggs, flour, baking powder, spinach, feta, mozzarella, salt, and pepper, mix to combine.
3. Pour 2 cups of water into the Instant Pot and place a rack into the pot (hang it onto the edges so it doesn't touch the water).
4. Cover the rack with baking paper.
5. Roll the mixture into rough ball shapes (it will be sloppy but do the best you can, they don't need to be perfect) and place the balls onto the baking paper-lined rack.
6. Secure the lid onto the pot and press the MANUAL button, adjust the temperature to HIGH, and adjust the time to 8 minutes.
7. Once the pot beeps, quick-release the pressure and remove the lid.
8. Place the bites onto a serving tray and serve with a dipping sauce such as garlic yogurt.

TIP: you may have to cook the bites in 2 batches to avoid the bites sticking together.

Bean Dip

Chop up some carrot, celery, and capsicum slices, get some tortilla chips, whip-up this bean dip and voila! A yummy starter, ready to go. Double the recipe if you've got lots of guests to feed.

Serves: about 6-8 as a starter for dipping
Time: approximately 35 minutes

Ingredients:
- 2 tins black beans, drained
- 2 tins red kidney beans, drained
- 1 tin navy beans, drained
- 2 onions, finely chopped
- 6 garlic cloves, finely chopped
- 1 tsp ground paprika
- ½ tsp chili powder
- 1 cup grated mozzarella
- Handful of chives, finely chopped

Method:
1. Drizzle some olive oil into the Instant Pot and press the SAUTE button, keep the temperature at NORMAL.
2. Add the onions and garlic to the pot and sauté until soft.
3. Add all of the beans, paprika, chili powder, mozzarella, ½ cup of water, salt, and pepper to the pot, stir to combine.
4. Secure the lid onto the pot and press the BEAN/CHILI button, adjust the time to 25 minutes.
5. Once the pot beeps, quick-release the pressure and remove the lid.
6. With a potato masher, mash the beans until smooth with a few chunks.
7. Spoon the dip into a serving bowl and sprinkle with chives!

Asparagus Tarts

Even people who think they don't like asparagus will adore these flaky, cheesy, and delicious tarts! This recipe requires the Instant Pot and the oven.

Serves: makes about 20 little tarts
Time: approximately 30 minutes

Ingredients:
- 1 packet store-bought puff pastry
- 15 asparagus spears, woody ends cut off
- 5 eggs, lightly beaten
- 1 spring onion (scallion), white part finely chopped
- 1 cup grated cheddar

Method:
1. Preheat the oven to 374 degrees Fahrenheit.
2. Pour 2 cups of water into the instant pot and place the steaming basket into the pot.
3. Place the asparagus into the basket and sprinkle with salt.
4. Secure the lid onto the pot and press the STEAM button, adjust the time to 3 minutes.
5. Grease a mini muffin tray (or 2 to allow for 20 tarts) with butter or oil spray.
6. Cut out 2 squares of pastry large enough to fit into the muffin tins with enough excess to fold over the top of the tarts once filled, line the muffin tins with pastry squares.
7. Once the Instant Pot beeps, quick-release the pressure and remove the lid, take the asparagus out of the basket and place on a board, cut the cooked asparagus into small pieces.
8. Place a few pieces of cooked asparagus into each pastry-lined muffin hole.
9. Pour the beaten egg over the asparagus then sprinkle with spring onions and grated cheese.
10. Place the trays in the oven to cook for about 10 minutes or until the egg has set and the cheese has melted!

Sticky Chicken Toothpick Meatballs

A meatball on a toothpick is a glorious thing, especially when it's covered in sticky sauce. These meatballs use minced chicken for a refreshing change.

Serves: makes about 30 meatballs
Time: approximately 30 minutes

Ingredients:
- 2 lb minced chicken
- 2 eggs, lightly beaten
- 1 cup breadcrumbs
- 2 spring onions (scallions), white part finely sliced
- 1/3 cup (about 3floz) soy sauce
- 3 tbsp honey
- 1 tsp sesame oil

Method:
1. In a large bowl, combine the minced chicken, eggs, breadcrumbs, scallions, salt, and pepper.
2. Drizzle some olive oil into the Instant Pot and press the SAUTE button, keep the temperature at NORMAL.
3. Roll the meatball mixture into 30 balls and place on a place next to the Instant Pot.
4. Cook the balls in about 3 batches, turning to ensure all surfaces of the meatballs become golden brown.
5. Once all of the meatballs are cooked, place them on a serving tray and poke a toothpick into each one.
6. Add the soy sauce, honey, and sesame oil to the instant pot and simmer for a couple of minutes on the SAUTE function until sticky.
7. Pour the sauce over the meatballs before serving!

Mini Chicken Salads in Cos Lettuce Cups

I love serving salads in cos lettuce cups! Not only is it cute and pretty, but it's very handy as you don't need to find lots of mini salad bowls. If you don't like to use dried apricots in your salads, simply leave them out.

Serves: makes about 15 mini salads
Time: approximately 30 minutes

Ingredients:
- 2 cos lettuces (you'll need 15 cup-shaped lettuce leaves)
- 1 cup (8fl oz) chicken stock
- 3 chicken breasts, skinless
- 3 tbsp mayonnaise
- 2 tbsp Greek yoghurt
- 12 dried apricots, finely chopped
- 2 spring onions (scallions), white part finely chopped
- 10 walnuts, roughly chopped

Method:
1. Rub the chicken breasts with olive oil, salt and pepper and place them into the Instant Pot with the chicken stock.
2. Secure the lid onto the pot and press the POULTRY button, keep the time at the default 15 minutes.
3. Once the pot beeps, quick-release the pressure and remove the lid, take the chicken breasts out and place them onto a board to rest for about 7 minutes.
4. Cut the chicken breasts into small pieces and place into a large bowl.
5. Add the mayonnaise, yoghurt, apricots, spring onions, walnuts, salt, and pepper to the bowl with the chicken, stir to thoroughly combine.
6. Lay the cos lettuce leaves out on your serving platter and fill each one with the chicken mixture.
7. Sneak a couple for yourself before serving!

Stuffed Capsicum Starters

Red capsicums turn into wonderful edible serving dishes when you fill them with yummy things such as mushrooms, ricotta cheese and almonds! I serve these as a first course or appetizer, as they are satisfying but not too filling.

Serves: 8 (1 stuffed capsicum half per serving)
Time: approximately 30 minutes

Ingredients:
- 4 red capsicums, halved, seeds and core removed
- 3 eggs
- 1 cup ricotta cheese
- ½ cup grated parmesan
- 4 large Portobello mushrooms, chopped into small pieces
- 1/3 cup roasted almonds, finely chopped
- Fresh parsley, finely chopped

Method:
1. In a medium-sized bowl, mix together the eggs, ricotta, parmesan, mushroom pieces, chopped almonds, salt, and pepper until combined.
2. Fill the capsicum halves with the filling mixture.
3. Pour 1 cup of water into the Instant Pot and place a rack into the pot.
4. Place the capsicum halves onto the rack and secure the lid onto the pot.
5. Press the POULTRY button and keep the time at the default 15 minutes.
6. Once the pot beeps, quick-release the pressure and remove the lid.
7. Take the stuffed capsicums out of the pot and place them on a serving dish, sprinkle with chopped parsley before serving!

Herb-Encrusted Cheese Balls

These decadent snacks are purely for cheese lovers. You only need one or two of these to satisfy your cravings for salty, cheesy goodness. I only make these for special occasions, as I don't think I would be able to stop myself from eating too many!

Serves: makes about 25 small cheese balls
Time: approximately 20 minutes

Ingredients:
- 10 oz cream cheese
- 3.5 oz brie, cut into small pieces
- ½ cup grated cheddar
- 1 cup ricotta cheese
- Fresh parsley, thyme, and mint finely chopped
- 1 cup breadcrumbs

Method:
1. In a medium-sized bowl, combine the cream cheese, brie, cheddar, ricotta, and a pinch of pepper (no salt as the cheeses are salty enough) until combined.
2. Mix together the herbs and breadcrumbs on a plate.
3. Roll the cheese mixture into 25 balls and roll them in the herb/breadcrumb mixture to coat.
4. Drizzle some olive oil into the Instant Pot and press the SAUTE button, keep the temperature at NORMAL.
5. Once the pot Is hot, place the balls carefully into the hot oil and fry them for a few minutes, turning a few times, until the outsides are golden and crispy.
6. Serve with toothpicks so they can be easily picked up and devoured!

Camembert-Stuffed Rice Bundles

Another appetizer recipe featuring cheese! I hope you aren't sick of cheese by now…surely not! These camembert-stuffed rice bundles are inspired by the Italian starter arancini. Serve with a tangy tomato relish and some toothpicks for easy eating.

Serves: makes about 20 bundles
Time: approximately 30 minutes

Ingredients:
- 2 cups dry Arborio (risotto) rice
- 1 egg, lightly beaten
- 4 cups chicken stock
- 1 wheel of camembert, about 7oz, chopped into 20 small pieces
- 1 cup bread crumbs

Method:
1. Cook the rice in the Instant Pot using the RICE function (it will automatically cook so you don't need to adjust anything), use chicken stock instead of water.
2. Once the pot beeps, quick-release the pressure and remove the lid.
3. Remove the rice from the pot and place into a large bowl to cool for a few minutes.
4. Add the egg and a sprinkling of salt and pepper to the rice, stir to combine.
5. Roll the rice mixture into 20 balls and press a piece of camembert into the center of each one, smoothing over any holes so the cheese is completely concealed.
6. Roll the balls in the breadcrumbs.
7. Drizzle some olive oil into your Instant Pot and press the SAUTE button, adjust the temperature to HIGH.
8. Once the pot is hot, place the balls into the hot oil and fry for a few minutes, turning so that every surface is golden and crispy.
9. Serve on a platter with some tangy relish!

Crostini with Thinly-Sliced Beef

Crostini are basically just slices of French bread which have been brushed with olive oil and toasted in the oven. These crostini are topped with mustard and sliced rare beef. Another lovely topping is salmon, cream cheese, and lemon slices.

Serves: 20 crostini
Time: approximately 25 minutes

Ingredients:

- 1 French bread stick, sliced into 20 slices
- 4 garlic cloves, crushed
- 1 large beef steak, sirloin is best!
- 2 tbsp wholegrain mustard

Method:

1. Preheat the oven to GRILL on MEDIUM heat.
2. Brush the French bread slices with olive oil and sprinkle each one with a small amount of crushed garlic and some salt.
3. Place the bread slices on an oven tray and grill them in the oven until golden.
4. Press the SAUTE button on your Instant Pot and adjust the temperature to HIGH.
5. Rub the steak with olive oil, salt, and pepper and place into the very hot pot.
6. Cook on both sides for about 2 minutes each, or until the steak is cooked to your likin (medium rare preferably).
7. Once the steak has cooked, leave on a board to rest for 5 minutes before thinly slicing.
8. Spread a small amount of mustard onto each crostini then top with a few strips of steak.
9. Drizzle the crostini with some olive oil and sprinkle some sea salt over the top for extra flair!

Mixed Nuts with Honey Soy Glaze

A mixture of almonds, pecans, walnuts, brazil nuts, and macadamia nuts coated in a salty-sweet mixture of soy sauce and honey. Place these on the table next time you host friends for drinks, or as a movie night snack!

Serves: 4 cups
Time: approximately 15 minutes

Ingredients:
- 4 cups mixed raw nuts
- ½ cup (4floz) soy sauce
- 4tbsp honey
- ½ tsp curry powder (optional, but it gives a lovely warm flavor)

Method:
1. Press the SAUTE button on your Instant Pot and keep the temperature at NORMAL.
2. Place the soy sauce, honey, ½ cup of water, and curry powder (if using) into the pot, stir to combine and bring to a gentle simmer.
3. Add the nuts to the pot and keep stirring as they gently toast and caramelize in the sauce.
4. Once the sauce becomes very thick and almost dry, take the coated nuts out of the pot and leave on a tray to cool.
5. Once the nuts are cool, place them in a bowl to be devoured by hungry nibblers! (But mostly by you, of course!).

Desserts

Finally, we come to my favorite section! I have a major sweet tooth and I'm not afraid to admit it. Desserts and sweet treats make life brighter and better in my opinion (In moderation, or not...)! The Instant Pot might not be the obvious appliance when it comes to making dessert, but it's actually a wonderful tool for sweet dishes. Here you will find fruity, chocolaty, creamy, and caramel-y desserts to enjoy.

Instant Pot Gingerbread Cheesecake

Cheesecake! And not just cheesecake...gingerbread cheesecake! The ginger comes from the base which is made from ginger biscuits, and the filling has a touch of ground ginger too. If you want to be extra fancy you can spread caramel sauce on the top before serving...

Serves: about 10 small slices
Time: approximately 1 hour

Ingredients:
- 9 oz ginger biscuits, crushed
- 4 oz butter, melted
- 17 oz plain cream cheese
- 9 oz sour cream
- 3 eggs
- ¾ cup sugar
- 1 tsp vanilla extract
- 1 tsp ground ginger

Method:
1. In a small bowl, mix together the crushed biscuits and melted butter, press into a greased and lined cake tin (ensure it fits into the Instant Pot first!).
2. In a large bowl, add the cream cheese, sour cream, eggs, sugar, vanilla, and ginger, beat with an electric egg beater until combined and smooth.
3. Pour the cream cheese mixture into the tin and spread over top of the biscuit base.
4. Pour 1 and a half cups of water into the Instant Pot and place a trivet into the pot.
5. Sit the cheesecake on top of the trivet and secure the lid onto the pot.
6. Press the MANUAL button, adjust the temperature to LOW, and adjust the time to 45 minutes.
7. Once the pot beeps, quick-release the pressure and remove the lid.
8. Very carefully, remove the tin from the pot and leave on a bench to cool before removing the cake and slicing!

TIP: a spring form cake tin works best, so you can simply unclip the tin and reveal the cake within, instead of having to awkwardly tip it upwards to get it out.

Lemon Tart with Whipped Cream

Lemon tart with freshly whipped cream on top. This tart manages to be refreshing and decadent all at the same time! You could use oranges instead of lemons if you can't find enough ripe lemons, but the tart won't be as sour (I LOVE the sourness).

Serves: about 8 medium slices
Time: approximately 1 hour and 30 minutes

Ingredients:
- 1 cup plain flour
- 3.5 oz butter
- ¼ cup sugar
- 1 egg yolk (for the pastry)
- 1 cup (8fl oz) heavy cream
- ½ cup (4fl oz) fresh lemon juice
- 4 eggs, lightly beaten (for the filling)
- 1/2 cup sugar

Method:
1. Prepare the tart tin by greasing the sides with butter and lining the bottom with baking paper (ensure the tin fits into the Instant Pot!), preheat the oven to 374 degrees Fahrenheit (this is to prebake the pastry case).
2. Place the flour, butter, sugar, and egg yolk into a food processor, add 1 tablespoon of cold water, blitz until the mixture gathers into a ball.
3. Take the pastry ball out of the food processor and place in the fridge for about 30 minutes.
4. In a medium-sized bowl, whisk together the cream, eggs, lemon juice, and sugar until smooth.
5. Roll the pastry out into a round circle until it's about 5mm thick and lay the pastry over the tin, pressing it into the corners and along the base, trim the edges if need be.
6. Prebake the pastry case by baking in the oven for 15 minutes.
7. Pour the lemon filling into the pastry case.
8. Pour 1 and a half cups of water into the Instant Pot and place a trivet into the pot, carefully place the tart tin on top of the trivet.
9. Secure the lid onto the pot and press the MANUAL button, adjust the temperature to LOW, and adjust the time to 45 minutes.
10. Once the pot beeps, quick-release the pressure and remove the lid.
11. Carefully take the tart out and leave to cool slightly before removing from the tin and slicing, serve with a cloud of whipped cream on top!

Rice Pudding with Pecans and Raisins

Rice pudding is like porridge for night time! This recipe uses raisins and pecans. I know not everyone likes raisins, so you can leave them out or swap them for something else such as dried apricots or cranberries.

Serves: 6
Time: approximately 30 minutes

Ingredients:
- 2 cups dry Arborio (risotto) rice
- ½ cup sugar
- ¼ cup brown sugar
- 3 cups full-fat milk
- ½ cup chopped pecans
- ¾ cup raisins
- 1 tsp cinnamon
- 1 tsp vanilla extract

Method:
1. Place the rice, sugars, milk, pecans, raisins, cinnamon, 2 cups of water, and vanilla extract into the Instant Pot, stir to combine.
2. Secure the lid onto the pot and press the MANUAL button, adjust the temperature to HIGH and set the time for 30 minutes.
3. Once the pot beeps, quick-release the pressure and remove the lid.
4. Give the rice pudding a good stir before serving.

Apple and Caramel Pie

An apple pie with caramel sauce hidden inside, hungry yet!? This pie is baked in the oven to ensure a golden and flaky pastry, but the apples are softened and caramelized in the Instant Pot.

Serves: about 8 medium slices
Time: approximately 1 hour

Ingredients:
- Store-bought pie crust (you can make your own from scratch, but I like to keep this pie as simple as I can!)
- 7-8 granny smith apples, peeled, cored, and cut into slices
- 3.5 oz butter
- ¾ cup brown sugar
- ½ cup (4fl oz) heavy cream
- 1 tsp cinnamon

Method:
1. Preheat the oven to 374 degrees Fahrenheit.
2. Prepare the pie tin by greasing the sides with butter, and lining the base with baking paper.
3. Roll out your store-bought pastry (or homemade) and line the pie tin, prick it with a fork, leave some pastry left over to cut into strips to create a lattice to go on top of the pie.
4. Press the SAUTE button on your Instant Pot and keep the temperature at NORMAL.
5. Add the butter, sugar, cream, cinnamon, and a pinch of salt to the pot, stir as it melts and begins to simmer.
6. Add the apples to the pot and stir to coat in caramel, allow them to simmer for about 10 minutes until they begin to soften.
7. Place the pastry-lined pie in the oven to pre-bake for about 12 minutes or until lightly golden, take out of the oven and set on the bench to be filled.
8. Place the caramelized apples into the pastry filling and place the pastry strips on top of the apples to create a lattice.
9. Place the pie back into the oven and bake for about 25-30 minutes until the lattice is golden brown.
10. Leave to cool on the bench for at least an hour before serving! (Oh, and serve with ice cream please!).

Chocolate and Brandy Sauce

This incredible sauce can be stored in the fridge until needed (up to a week). When the time comes to eat the sauce, simply melt it in the microwave in short increments until warm and oozy. The brandy is very subtle, but it gives a very sophisticated flavor.

Serves: makes 1 large bottle of sauce
Time: approximately 25 minutes

Ingredients:
- 9 oz dark chocolate, broken into chunks
- 1 cup (8fl oz) heavy cream
- 1 tbsp sugar
- 2 tbsp brandy

Method:
1. Place the chocolate, cream, sugar, and brandy into your Instant Pot and press the SAUTE button, adjust the temperature to LOW.
2. Keep stirring the sauce as the chocolate melts, to stop it from catching.
3. Continue to stir the sauce as it becomes smooth, thick, and glossy.
4. If it's too thick for your liking, add more cream.
5. Once the sauce has reached the consistency you prefer, pour it into a glass bottle or jar, allow it to cool, then store it in the fridge.
6. Pour over ice cream, cake, or sneak spoonsful when no one is looking!

Apple and Berry Crumble with White Chocolate Surprise

I love to add "surprises" to my classic desserts. Usually this just means I hide chocolate, or caramel sauce somewhere in the dessert, to be found when eaten! This apple and berry crumble has a white chocolate surprise hiding just beneath the crumble.

Serves: 6-8
Time: approximately 45 minutes

Ingredients:
- 2 cups plain flour
- ¾ cup sugar
- ¼ cup brown sugar
- 7 oz butter, cut into cubes
- ½ tsp baking powder
- 1 tsp cinnamon
- 7 granny smith apples, peeled, cored, and sliced
- 1 ½ cups frozen berries
- 7 oz white chocolate, chopped into small pieces

Method:
1. Place the flour, sugars, butter, baking powder, and cinnamon into a large bowl, rub the butter into the dry ingredients until the mixture takes on a sandy, crumbly texture.
2. In a round, heat-proof dish, place the sliced apples and frozen berries, sprinkle 1tbsp water over the top.
3. Scatter the white chocolate over the fruit, then sprinkle the crumble mixture over the top.
4. Pour 1 and a half cups of water into the Instant Pot and place a trivet into the pot.
5. Place the crumble on top of the trivet and secure the lid onto the pot.
6. Press the MANUAL button and adjust the temperature to HIGH, adjust the time to 40 minutes.
7. Once the pot beeps, quick-release the pressure and remove the lid.
8. Take the crumble out of the pot and serve immediately, with ice cream and/or pouring cream!

Caramel and Ginger Sauce

Caramel sauce is yummy enough, but adding ginger makes it perfect for Winter desserts, or simply pouring over ice cream or poached fruit.

Serves: makes 1 large bottle or jar of sauce
Time: approximately 20 minutes

Ingredients:
- 5 oz butter
- 1 ½ cups (12fl oz) heavy cream
- ¾ cups brown sugar
- 1 tsp ground ginger

Method:
1. Place the butter, cream, sugar, and ginger into your Instant Pot.
2. Press the SAUTE button and adjust the temperature to LOW.
3. Stir the sauce as the butter melts and the sauce begins to simmer.
4. Leave to simmer for about 5 minutes, checking regularly to prevent catching.
5. Once the sauce is smooth and thick, serve right away, or store in the fridge in a glass jar or bottle!

Instant Pot Vanilla Peaches

Fresh, in-season peaches can be made into so many wonderful desserts. One of my favorite peach desserts is a simple poached peach, with lovely vanilla syrup. Of course, a scoop of vanilla ice cream on the side is mandatory!

Serves: makes 4 peaches, but you can add more if need be
Time: approximately 40 minutes

Ingredients:
- 4 ripe peaches
- 1/3 cup sugar
- 1 tbsp vanilla extract
- 1 lemon

Method:
1. Place the sugar, vanilla extract, juice and rind of 1 lemon, and 1 cup of water into your Instant Pot, stir to combine.
2. Place the peaches into the pot and spoon the sugar/water mixture over them to coat.
3. Secure the lid onto the pot and press the BEAN/CHILI button, keep the temperature at the default 30 minutes.
4. Once the pot beeps, quick-release the pressure and remove the lid.
5. Serve the peaches hot, with a big spoonful of vanilla syrup.

Mango, Raspberry, and Coconut Custard

Coconut custard is a tropical take on regular custard. It can be eaten alone, or as a sauce on top of other cakes and desserts. This recipe features mango and raspberries...the flavor combination is pretty mind blowing!

Serves: about 6
Time: approximately 35 minutes

Ingredients:
- 2 cups (16fl oz) coconut milk
- 1 cup full-fat cow's milk
- ½ cup sugar
- 3 egg yolks =
- 1 tsp vanilla extract
- 1 cup mango flesh, chopped into chunks
- 1 cup frozen raspberries

Method:
1. Pour 2 cups of water into the Instant pot and place a trivet into the pot.
2. In a medium-sized, heat-proof bowl, add the coconut milk, cow's milk, sugar, egg yolks, and vanilla, whisk to combine.
3. Stir the mango and raspberries through the mixture.
4. Place the bowl on top of the trivet inside the pot.
5. Secure the lid onto the pot and press the manual button, adjust the temperature to HIGH and adjust the time to 30 minutes.
6. Once the pot beeps, quick-release the pressure and remove the lid.
7. Stir the custard, it might be a bit lumpy, but keep stirring until it becomes smooth.
8. Serve however you like!

Chocolate and Almond Truffles

Truffles make a lovely handmade gift or simple dessert for special occasions. Make a batch of these in the lead-up to Christmas time so you can take little boxes of them to dinner parties as a present for the host! (Or keep them for yourself and your family...I would).

Serves: makes about 20 truffles
Time: approximately 2 hours including cooling

Ingredients:
- 9 oz dark chocolate
- 1 cup (8fl oz) heavy cream
- ½ cup sugar
- 1 cup toasted almonds, finely chopped
- 1 tbsp brandy, rum, or whisky
- ½ cup cocoa powder or icing sugar

Method:
1. Place the chocolate, cream, sugar, almonds, and liquor into the Instant Pot.
2. Press the SAUTE button and adjust the temperature to LOW.
3. Stir the ingredients as the chocolate melts, and keep stirring until it comes together to form a smooth, sauce-like mixture.
4. Allow to simmer for about 5 minutes, keeping an eye on it to make sure it doesn't catch and burn.
5. Pour the chocolate mixture into a bowl and place into the fridge to cool and become firm.
6. Once the mixture is cool and hard, use a spoon to scoop golf ball-sized amounts, roll into a smooth ball.
7. Roll the balls into cocoa or icing sugar (or both!) to finish.
8. Store the truffles in the fridge.

Marshmallow, Chocolate, and Coconut Bundles

Our last sweet recipe is a fun and whimsical treat. Chocolate, marshmallow, and coconut all bundled together to create an addictive sweet snack or dessert. I like to make these when I am going to parties where I know there will be kids there, as little ones just adore these!

Serves: makes about 20 bundles
Time: approximately 2 hours including cooling

Ingredients:

- 9 oz dark chocolate, broken into small pieces
- 4 oz milk chocolate, broken into small pieces
- 2 cups mini marshmallows
- 2.5 oz butter
- 1 cup shredded coconut

Method:

1. Place the dark chocolate, milk chocolate, marshmallows, butter, and coconut into your Instant Pot.
2. Press the SAUTE button and adjust the temperature to LOW.
3. Keep stirring as the chocolate, butter, and marshmallows melt.
4. Once all of the ingredients have melted together, place tablespoon-sized dollops of mixture onto a paper-lined tray.
5. Place the tray into the fridge to allow the bundles to set and harden.
6. Once the bundles have set and hardened, place them in an airtight container to store in the fridge before serving!

Conclusion

I bet you are a complete Instant Pot expert by now! I hope you've found some new favorites among these recipes, and some inspiration to create new recipes of your own. Remember, you can modify, adapt, and customize all of these recipes to suit your taste! There are no rules when it comes to home cooking, as long as you're enjoying the process and more importantly...enjoying the tasty results.

Let your Instant Pot be your little kitchen buddy. When you're pressed for time, choose recipes which the Instant Pot can cook in an...instant. Recipes which utilize the Soup, Beans, or Poultry function are often super quick and easy. Or, if you want to come home to a meal as you just know you won't be in the mood for cooking after work, use the Slow Cook function!

Remember to keep your Instant Pot clean by rinsing out the inner pot, wiping down the outer casing, and making sure the inner base (under the inner pot) is clean and dry.

Go ahead and start cooking!

Made in the USA
Columbia, SC
17 December 2017